FINSBURY PARK *TO* ALEXANDRA PALACE

J. E. CONNOR

Series editor Vic Mitchell

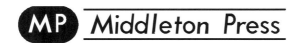
MP Middleton Press

Cover picture: A class N2 0-6-2T steams into Muswell Hill with a Finsbury Park - Alexandra Palace train, shortly before the line closed in 1954. (Lens of Sutton)

Published November 1997

ISBN 1 901706 028

© *Middleton Press 1997*

Cover design - Deborah Goodridge

Published by Middleton Press
      Easebourne Lane
      Midhurst
      West Sussex
      GU29 9AZ
      Tel: 01730 813169
      Fax: 01730 812601

Typesetting and layout - London Railway Record

Printed & bound by Biddles Ltd,
      Guildford and Kings Lynn

CONTENTS

GEOGRAPHICAL SETTING

Situated to the north-west of Finsbury Park, the area contains the populous suburbs of Crouch End, Highgate and Muswell Hill. The district is fairly hilly, hence it is often described as the Northern Heights. All maps are to the scale of 25ins to 1 mile.

ACKNOWLEDGMENTS

I am very grateful for assistance received from those mentioned in the photographic credits, and also help given by J.L.Crook, G.W.Goslin, R.J.Harley and L.A.Heath Humphrys, together with my ever-supportive trio, Tricia, Barbie and son, Charlie.

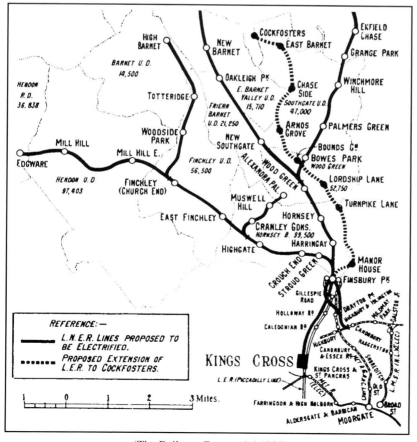

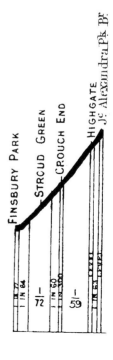

(The Railway Gazette 4.4.1930)

HISTORICAL BACKGROUND
J. Derrick

The branch owed its origins to the Edgware, Highgate & London Railway which obtained an Act in 1862 to construct a line from the 1850 Great Northern Railway route at Seven Sisters Road (later Finsbury Park) to link with Finchley and Edgware. An agreement was reached whereby the main line company would provide staff, and operate services in return for 50% of the gross receipts.

Authorisation came in 1864, both for the main route to Edgware, and a 1mile 11chain double track branch from Highgate to Muswell Hill, which was close to the new Alexandra Palace then under construction. In 1866, a further Act was passed, which allowed the Muswell Hill Estate Company, who owned the land, to extend the line into the grounds of Alexandra Park, and terminate at a station adjoining the north-western facade of the Palace itself. This was to be known as the Muswell Hill & Palace Railway, and was independent of the EH&L. The main route to Edgware was brought into use from 22nd August 1867, but although the necessary land for the branch had been acquired, construction did not start until the closing months of 1871. However, as it was of no great length, the work was soon completed, and the line from Highgate opened with the Palace on 24th May 1873.

As had been agreed, the line was worked throughout by the Great Northern, as neither the EH&LR nor the Muswell Hill & Palace Railway owned any locomotives or stock. The line was to prove popular, as it

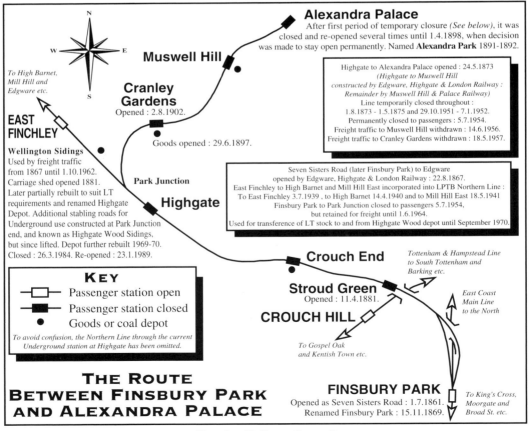

THE ROUTE BETWEEN FINSBURY PARK AND ALEXANDRA PALACE

Alexandra Palace
After first period of temporary closure (See below), it was closed and re-opened several times until 1.4.1898, when decision was made to stay open permanently. Named **Alexandra Park** 1891-1892.

Highgate to Alexandra Palace opened : 24.5.1873
(Highgate to Muswell Hill
constructed by Edgware, Highgate & London Railway :
Remainder by Muswell Hill & Palace Railway)
Line temporarily closed throughout :
1.8.1873 - 1.5.1875 and 29.10.1951 - 7.1.1952.
Permanently closed to passengers : 5.7.1954.
Freight traffic to Muswell Hill withdrawn : 14.6.1956.
Freight traffic to Cranley Gardens withdrawn : 18.5.1957.

Muswell Hill

Cranley Gardens
Opened : 2.8.1902.

Goods opened : 29.6.1897.

To High Barnet, Mill Hill and Edgware etc.

EAST FINCHLEY

Wellington Sidings
Used by freight traffic from 1867 until 1.10.1962. Carriage shed opened 1881. Later partially rebuilt to suit LT requirements and renamed Highgate Depot. Additional stabling roads for Underground use constructed at Park Junction end, and known as Highgate Wood Sidings, but since lifted. Depot further rebuilt 1969-70. Closed : 26.3.1984. Re-opened : 23.1.1989.

Park Junction

Highgate

Seven Sisters Road (later Finsbury Park) to Edgware opened by Edgware, Highgate & London Railway : 22.8.1867.
East Finchley to High Barnet and Mill Hill East incorporated into LPTB Northern Line :
To East Finchley 3.7.1939 , to High Barnet 14.4.1940 and to Mill Hill East 18.5.1941
Finsbury Park to Park Junction closed to passengers 5.7.1954,
but retained for freight until 1.6.1964.
Used for transference of LT stock to and from Highgate Wood depot until September 1970.

Crouch End

Tottenham & Hampstead Line to South Tottenham and Barking etc.

Stroud Green
Opened : 11.4.1881.

CROUCH HILL

East Coast Main Line to the North

To Gospel Oak and Kentish Town etc.

KEY
— Passenger station open
— Passenger station closed
● Goods or coal depot

To avoid confusion, the Northern Line through the current Underground station at Highgate has been omitted.

FINSBURY PARK
Opened as Seven Sisters Road : 1.7.1861.
Renamed Finsbury Park : 15.11.1869.

To King's Cross, Moorgate and Broad St. etc.

(London Railway Record)

offered the most convenient means of travelling from central London to the Palace. On Whit Monday 1873, 60,000 visitors were recorded, but sadly this success was doomed for an early setback.

Tragedy struck the Palace on Monday 9th June 1873, when it was totally gutted by fire. The Great Northern did their best to assist during the blaze, and sent two fire appliances by rail from King's Cross. These arrived on the scene before the local brigade, but to no avail, as the inferno was so fierce that within just ninety minutes the premises were virtually destroyed.

For a short while, a reduced service of seven trains each way was operated for sightseers who found fascination in the blackened ruin. However, the novelty proved to be short lived, and branch passenger workings were suspended from 1st August 1873, leaving just a daily goods train to Muswell Hill which ran if required.

Rebuilding the Palace was soon under way, with the first new bricks being laid on 10th October 1873, but it took the best part of two years to complete, and was not ready for opening until May Day 1875.

When it finally reopened, the trains were restored, with the previous GNR services augmented by North London Railway workings which reached the branch by way of the Canonbury-Finsbury Park spur, brought into passenger use earlier that year.

A total of 21,000 people visited the Palace on the day it reopened, and the majority of these arrived by rail. Much larger crowds materialised on the following Whit Monday, when 94,000 attended, but the boom was not to last, and by the following year the owners were in financial trouble.

For the rest of its existence, the fortunes of Alexandra Palace station were inextricably linked with those of the Palace itself, and it was closed on a number of occasions due to insufficient demand. The Great Northern nevertheless wanted to encourage residential traffic to the line, and when it reopened the terminus in March 1891 after one of its periods of disuse, it was given the name Alexandra Park, to emphasise the area rather than the Palace. Unfortunately the hoped-for traffic failed to materialise, and it was closed again in the April of the following year.

No doubt to promote confidence to would-be commuters, the GNR eventually made an agreement with the MH&PR whereby the station should remain open on a permanent basis, and therefore from 1898 it came back into full use with its original name restored.

Suburban growth ensured that traffic on the remainder of the branch was rather more successful, and even warranted the opening of an additional station at Cranley Gardens in 1902. However although the route between Muswell Hill and central London became busy, receipts from the terminus remained comparatively poor. A survey held by the GNR in March 1914 revealed that only 4,392 passengers had used Alexandra Palace station that month, compared with 12,948 at Cranley Gardens and 20,051 at Muswell Hill.

In 1911, the Muswell Hill & Palace Railway, which had surprisingly managed to remain nominally independent, was finally bought by the GNR at a cost of £18,416, and was therefore absolved from paying out 5% interest on £1,584, which the GNR had incurred on station improvements.

Just as the line's prospects were starting to improve, its traffic began to be eroded by competition from other forms of transport. From 6th December 1905, electric trams were introduced from Turnpike Lane to the foot of Muswell Hill, and through to the west side of the Palace itself. 11th April saw trams from Wood Green to the east side of Alexandra Palace, whilst 22nd June 1907 brought the opening of the Hampstead Tube line to Highgate, which was soon linked by bus to Muswell Hill. Both Alexandra Palace tram routes were served by single-deck cars, and those which operated from Turnpike Lane ran over reserved track through the park. By the outbreak of World War 1, the London General Omnibus Company was working a very frequent service of single deckers on route 111 between Finsbury Park, Crouch End and Muswell Hill, and offered through bookings onto the Underground system. The Great Northern responded to the threat by taking the LGOC to court on the grounds that their buses were causing an excessive strain on the overbridges at Crouch End and Cranley Gardens, but other than restricting the size of vehicles used, this did little to restrain the opposition. Although the number of passengers carried was dictated by the capacity of the bus, the LGOC was undaunted, and simply overcame the matter by operating more vehicles. Cleaner, more modern forms of transport were gaining in public esteem, whilst grimy and less efficient steam hauled trains were falling from favour. A journey between Alexandra Palace and Finsbury Park took fifteen minutes, with an extra two minutes allowed in the opposite direction to allow for the slog up the hills towards Highgate. At one time trains were operated from the branch onto the South Eastern & Chatham Railway by way of the Metropolitan Widened Lines and Snow Hill, but such services fell foul of tram, tube and bus competition, and were eventually withdrawn.

The onset of war brought the inevitable cuts, with off-peak workings over the line being replaced by a shuttle to and from Finsbury Park after 11th January 1915. All North London trains, outside rush hours, were also taken off, and the branch Sunday services were axed from 1st October of the same year.

Alexandra Park was temporarily used as a camp for German prisoners of war, and latterly accommodated Belgian refugees. The Germans were conveyed in military vehicles, but the Belgians were transported by rail and tram.

With the end of hostilities, full services were eventually restored, but although the off-peak North London Line trains reappeared, they were soon withdrawn.

World War 1 had left much of the nation's railways in a run-down condition, and clearly something needed to be done to improve matters. Therefore an Act was passed by Parliament in 1921 which brought the majority of individual companies under the control of four main groups. This grouping officially took place on 1st January 1923, when the lines radiating from King's Cross became part of the London & North Eastern Railway.

Even the two Metropolitan Electric Tramway routes serving the Palace had proved a failure, having been hopelessly uneconomic to operate. They nevertheless survived the formation of the London Passenger Transport Board in 1933, and were not withdrawn until 23rd February 1938.

With the general decline in patronage, the prospects for the LNER Alexandra Palace branch now appeared very bleak indeed, but possible salvation was offered by a New Works Plan of 1935, which included a scheme for the London Passenger Transport Board to take over all ex-GNR Northern Heights routes, and incorporate them into the Underground system.

It was intended to extend the Northern City Line from Moorgate to new high level platforms at Finsbury Park, then over LNER metals to Alexandra Palace, High Barnet and Edgware. The scheme envisaged a peak period service of fourteen trains an hour between Finsbury Park and Highgate, with half of these continuing to Alexandra Palace.

The Northern Heights lines started to be included on LPTB publicity material, and from 1938 they were shown on pocket Underground maps, together with an extension beyond Edgware to Bushey Heath. This situation continued into the early war years, and on Map No.3 of 1939, beneath the banner headline 'New In London', it was announced that tube trains were expected to be up and running on the Alexandra Palace branch by the autumn of 1940.

In the meantime however, the line was to remain served by steam trains until the work had been completed for the transition.

Northern Line electrics reached East Finchley on 3rd July 1939, although they had to run non-stop through the new underground platforms at Highgate which were not ready for full public use until 19th January 1941. Despite the conditions imposed by war, further extension work was carried out, but after reaching High Barnet and Mill Hill East, it slowly ground to a halt, and various unfinished tasks were mothballed for the duration.

Following electrification, the steam trains which formerly served High Barnet were cut back to East Finchley, but this practice ceased after March 1941 when they were diverted to Alexandra Palace instead. Sadly, this new improved service on the branch proved short lived, as from 7th September 1942, all through trains were withdrawn, and replaced by a meagre peak only shuttle, which ran three times an hour. Services ceased after 7pm on weekdays and from 5pm on Saturdays

When the war ended, thought was again given to continuing electrification work, but with the branch service now very run down, it was deemed rather pointless. After 1941, the Alexandra Palace line ceased to be shown on Underground maps, although it was to reappear in 1946. It was last featured in 1950, and then vanished for good.

Before the work ceased a great deal had been done, but abandoned before it could be put to use. Ramps were constructed, or partially constructed at Finsbury Park to connect the Northern City Line with the high level tracks, but again these were were left unfinished. Work at this end also included a new signal box at Drayton Park, with was sited at the country end of the station, and adjoined the southbound ramp. When the Northern City Line was eventually electrified by British Rail in 1976, these ramps were modified to suit main line height trains, and finally brought into use.

Once again, the cruel affects of a world war had resulted in a railway system which was in poor condition, and in need of government assistance. Therefore, a nationalisation scheme was introduced, and from 1st January 1948, the Alexandra Palace line became part of the Eastern Region of British Railways.

Services on the branch were suspended for economy reasons from 29th October 1951, and it was obvious that the end was not far off. After a degree of local pressure, the service was reinstated from 7th January 1952, but the infrequent and often unreliable trains did little to attract custom.

Closure was announced in 1953, together with a statement that the passenger numbers did not justify the cost of electrification. The service therefore only had a few months to go, with two-coach steam trains destined to shuttle to and fro until the end, instead of the clean, efficient tube trains, which until a few years earlier were expected to become a reality.

The last public train ran on 3rd July 1954, formed not of the usual two-car set, but strengthened to eight vehicles to accommodate the crowds of enthusiasts and other interested people who wanted to bid their farewells.

In the Autumn of 1954, a body was set up called The North London Passengers Protection Association Ltd, which intended to reopen the line, and operate it with ex-Great Western railcars. Their scheme would have pre-dated the first standard gauge preserved line by four years, but their efforts were unfortunately doomed to failure,

Alexandra Palace station dealt with passenger traffic only, and therefore closed completely, but freight continued to Muswell Hill until 14th June 1956, and Cranley Gardens until 18th May the following year.

The conductor rails on the section from Highgate to Alexandra Palace were removed between January 1954 and February 1955, but much of the lineside cabling remained. The track on the branch was lifted by early 1958, but that between Finsbury Park and Highgate was used until 1964 by freight trains to and from Edgware.

There were also transfer trips of tube stock between Highgate Wood sidings and Drayton Park, which were hauled by London Transport battery locomotives. These eventually ceased in the autumn of 1970 due to the poor condition of the station bridge at Crouch End, and the flyover above the main line at Finsbury Park. The track was lifted in January 1972, and the flyover demolished later the same year.

Much of the former trackbed has been converted into a public footpath known as The Parkland Walk, and has become so countrified that visiting strangers would find it difficult to believe that they were only about three miles from Kings Cross.

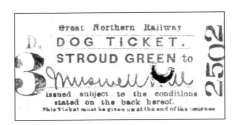

PASSENGER SERVICES

The initial timetable showed eighteen trains each way. By 1876, the figure had risen to twenty, but there was no service on Sundays. In the mid-1880s, the branch saw twenty-four trains, but they did not serve Alexandra Palace until mid-morning. A decade later, when Muswell Hill was being used as the terminus, there were thirty trips on the branch.

By 1910, the service amounted to fifty-two trains each way, although not all served the terminus. Of these, forty-one were operated by the GNR, whilst the others were provided by the North London. The earliest morning train from Muswell Hill departed for central London at 7.14am, whilst the last down train arrived there at sixteen minutes past midnight. At this time, there were Sunday trains as far as Muswell Hill, with one arriving at 9.56am, and a further nine in the afternoon.

The wartime economies meant a reduction to thirty-nine local trips in 1917, which operated on weekdays only.

Sunday workings over the branch between Highgate and Alexandra Palace were brought back from 1st September 1925, but there was little demand, and they were taken off again within five years.

In 1939, there were forty-three up trains throughout the day, spread out between 7.10am and 11.12pm, two of which ran to Broad Street, whilst the others served King's Cross or Moorgate.

With the coming of World War II, the branch saw further cuts, with through traffic to and from Moorgate and Broad Street being suspended from 10th September 1939. The rush-hour services onto the North London line were restored on 4th December 1939, but taken off completely from the following 3rd October, due to air-raid damage on the approaches to Broad Street.

From 1942 until closure, the branch was only served during the Monday-Friday peak periods, with trains running on Saturdays in the early morning and during the afternoon. During this period there was usually a total of about fifteen trains each day.

FINSBURY PARK

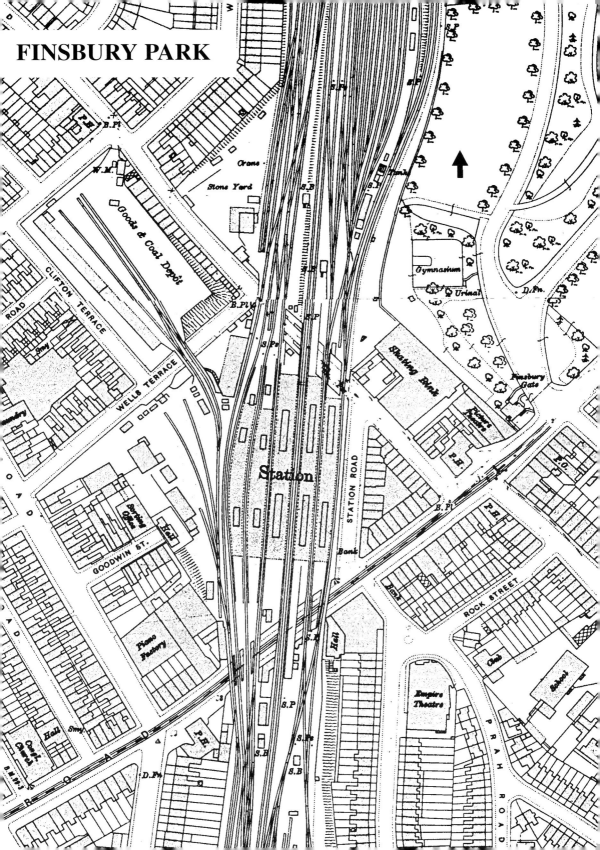

The station was opened as Seven Sisters Road on 1st July 1861, and enlarged six years later. It was renamed Finsbury Park from 15th November 1869, and totally rebuilt in 1874, when a subway replaced an earlier footbridge as means of access between platforms. This was enlarged in 1889, and joined by an additional subway which ran parallel at a higher level in 1894. Further alterations took place in 1904, when lifts and stairways were constructed to link the station with the new Great Northern & City tube line underneath. A similar arrangement was made for access to the Great Northern Piccadilly & Brompton Railway, which opened in 1906, with additional stairways and lifts being installed to provide an interchange facility. Both lots of lifts were soon taken out of public use and replaced by stairs, although one of those leading to the GN&C station remained available for staff purposes until 1968. An additional island platform was constructed on the down side in 1912, and later served the Alexandra Palace branch shuttles until their demise in 1954.

1. Here we look west along Seven Sisters Road in February 1939, with the corner of Station Road on the extreme right. Reconditioned E/1 tramcar No.1260 has just passed beneath the bridge, working on route 53 to Aldgate. *(Enfield & Wood Green Tramways (Middleton Press) contains further information and also includes the routes to* *Alexandra Palace.)* Early in the following month, this route was converted to trolleybuses, and renumbered 653. It lasted in this form until January 1961, when the trolleys were replaced by Routemasters, and the number changed to 253. The enamel sign on the wall directs passengers to both the LNER premises and the two tube lines. (British Rail)

2.   The street level entrance to Finsbury Park faced onto Station Road. Soon after this view was taken in February 1939, the frontage was demolished in readiness for rebuilding. (British Rail)

3.   A contemporary artist's impression shows how the rebuilt station was intended to look. All work on this project ceased during World War II, and was never resumed. (British Rail)

4.   On entering the station, passengers would purchase their tickets from the street level booking office, then walk through to a subway. From here, they ascended to another subway which was connected to the platforms by means of stairways. This view dates from 1952. (British Rail)

6.   Ex GNR class C12 4-4-2T No.7374 stands at Finsbury Park Platform 10 with the branch shuttle in July 1950. Somebody clearly thought that the service should be named, and therefore has chalked 'The Alexandra Palace Limited' on the smokebox door! (British Rail)

A northward view in the 1930s includes the island platform 9/10 to the extreme left. This was added in 1912, and was later used by the branch shuttle services. (Stations UK)

7.   In 1942, some ex-Great Central class F2 2-4-2Ts were transferred to King's Cross motive power depot for working the Alexandra Palace shuttle service. Here one of the class awaits departure from Finsbury Park with her two-car push-pull set in early BR days. These locomotives became a familiar sight on the Northern Heights, and remained on the branch until 1950, when the last of them was withdrawn for scrap. (Lens of Sutton)

9.   Platforms 9 and 10, looking north a little over a decade after the last regular passenger train ran to Alexandra Palace. It was the last part of the station to retain a full set of awnings, and remained in use until 22nd January 1973. (J.E. Connor)

Enthusiasts jostle to photograph N2/1 No.69519 after hauling the last regular passenger train from Alexandra Palace to Finsbury Park on 3rd July 1954. (Stephenson Locomotive Society)

10.   Looking from the station in 1968, we see the down line to Highgate ascending behind No.
signal box on the left. This box closed on 27th April 1975, and together with No.6, which is seen t
the right, has long since disappeared. (Robert Humm Collection)

12. We look north in 1992, and find that some pre-grouping buildings remained, but
they had been heavily rationalised by that time. (J.E. Connor)

11. The demolition of the structures on platforms 9 & 10 was recorded on 28th January 1973. (J.L.Crook)

LONDON, FINSBURY PARK, HIGHGATE, FINCHLEY, HIGH BARNET, EDGWARE

Week Days.

Fares, see p. 119.	gov	gov	gov	gov	gov	gov	gov	gov	gov	gov	gov	gov	gov	¶	gov	mrn	gov	gov	gov	gov	gov
Victoria....dep									7 4		7 50	8 5		8 5				8 26	8 48	9 15		9 53
Ludgate Hill „									7 38		8 25	8 38		8 43				9 7	9 24	9 50		9 54 10
Moorgate St. „		6 0			7 2		7 2			8 8		8 34	8 34		8 48			9 15	9 32	9 43		10 1 10
Aldersgate St. „		6 2			7 4		7 4			8 10		8 36	8 36		8 50			9 17	9 34	9 45		10 3 10
Farringdon St. „		6 4			7 6		7 6			8 12		8 38	8 42		8 52			9 19	9 36	9 54		10 5 10
King's C. (Mt) dp 4 28		6 8			7 10		7 10			8 16		8 42	8 46		8 56			9 23	9 40	9 58		10 9 10
(G.N.) „ 5-15	5 30	6 20		7 10	7 20		7 40		8 5	8 21		8 48	9 0		9 10			9 30	9 50	10 4		10 30 10
Holloway... „	5 35	6 25		7 15	7 25		7 45		8 10	8 26		8 53						9 35	9 55	10 9		10 35 10
Broad St..dep		6 32 6 42			7 12		7 47			8 32		8 52			9 29						10 7	
Shoreditch „		6 35 6 45			7 15		7 50			8 35		8 55			9 5	9 20					1010	
Haggrston „		6 37 6 47			7 17		7 52			8 37		8 57			9 7	9 22					1012	
Dalston „		6 40 6 51			7 19		7 54			8 39		8 59			9 9	9 24					1015	
Canonbury „		6 43 6 54			7 22		7 57			8 42					9 12	9 27					1018	
Finsbury Park	5 38 6 28 6 48 6 59		7 18 7 23	7 28 7 48	8 1 8 14	8 29 8 46	8 56	8 9	9 6	9 17	9 20	9 31	9 39	9 58	1012	1022	1038	10				
Crouch End „		5 38 6 28		6 52	7 22		7 32 7 52	8 -58	8 18 8 33		9 0		9 10			9 35	9 43	10 2	1016		10	
Highgate.... „		6 56		7 26		7 36 7 56	8 9 8 22	8 37		9 4		9 14			9 39	9 47	10 6	1020		10	
Muswell Hill „							8 41							9 53		1025		10	
Alexndra Pa „							8 44							9 56		1028		11	
East End, Finchly		7 0		7 30		7 40 8 0 8 13 8 26		9 8		9 18		9 43		1010			10	
Finchley.... „		7 4		7 34		7 44 8 4 8 17 8 30		9 12		9 22		9 47		1014			10	
Torrington Pk		7 8		7 38		7 48 8 8 8 21 8 34		9 16		9 26		9 51		1018			10	
Totteridge 2 „		7 12		7 42		7 52 8 12 8 25 8 38		9 20		9 30		9 55		1022			10	
High Brnet arr		7 17		7 47		7 57 8 17 8 30 8 42		9 25		9 35		10 0		1027			10	
Mill Hill.... „						8 11	8 45		9 28					1019				
Edgware.. arr						8 17	8 51		9 34					1025				
Hornsey....	5 43 6 33		7 4	7 33			8 51		9 22 9 28		9 25		1027 1043				
Wood Grn 3 [Hatch	5 46 6 36		7 7	7 36			8 54		9 27 9 33				1030 1046				
Southgate & Colney	5 51 6 41		7 12	7 41			8 58		9 33 9 39				1035 1051				
Oakleigh Pk, Whet	c	c		7 18	7 47			9 4		9 36 9 42				1041 c				
Barnet..[stone	6 0 6 50		7 21	7 50			9 7		9 46				1044 11 0				
Potters Bar [209					8 0				9 54				1110				
Hatfield 126,					8 13				b				1123				
Welwyn....					8 22				b				1132				
Stevenage [209					8 33				b				1143				
Hitchin 124, ar 5 58					8 41			9 48				1150				

Week Days. (Continued.)

Victoria....dep	1 45	1 45	1 45			2 35	2 50	2 50	3 0		3 0	3 40		3 40	3 55		3 55		4 23		4 23		4 23	4 53
Ludgate Hill „	2 19	2 19	2 19		2 58	3 10	3 25	3 23	3 38		3 56	4 13		4 26	4 26		4 56		4 56		4 56	5 8 5
Moorgate St. „	2 27	2 27	2 27		3 6	3 6	3 27	3 27		4 3	4 3	4 20	4 38	4 38		4 38	5 7		5 7		5 7 5 20 5
AldersgateSt. „	2 29	2 29	2 29		3 8	3 8	3 29	3 29		4 5	4 5	4 22	4 40	4 40		5 0	5 9		5 9		5 9 5 22 5
FarringdonSt „	2 31	2 31	2 31		3 10	3 14	3 31	3 31	3 42	4 7	4 17	4 24	4 42	4 42		5 2	5 13		5 13		5 13 5 26 5
King's C.(Mt) „	2 35	2 35	2 35		3 14	3 18	3 35	3 35	3 46	4 11	4 21	4 28	4 46	4 46		5 5	5 10	5 15	5 20		5 30 5 33 5
(G.N.) „	2 50	3 0	3		3 23	3 26	3 42	3 50	3 55	4 20	4 28	4 35	5 0		5 5	5 10	5 15	5 20	5 25		5 38 5
Holloway... „	2 55		3 8		3 28	3 31	3 47		4 0		4 33	4 40			5 15	5 20	5 25				5 38 5
Broad St. dep			3 12					4 7			4 27		4 47		5 2				5 17		
Shoreditch „			3 15					4 10			4 30		4 50		5 5				5 20		
Haggerston „			3 17					4 12			4 32		4 52		5 7				5 22		
Dalston Jn „			3 19					4 15			4 35		4 55		5 9				5 25		
Canonbury „			3 22					4 18			4 38		4 58		5 12				5 28		
Finsbury Park	2 59	3 7	3 12	3 27	3 31	3 34	3 50	3 58	4 3	4 22	4 27	4 37	4 43	4 43		5 5	5 12	5 17	5 18	5 24	5 28 5 33 5 37 5 41
Crouch End „	3 2		3 16	3 13	3 36		3 54		4 26		4 41		5 7		5 21		5 28	5 32			5
Highgate.... „	3 6		3 20	3 35	3 40		3 58		4 30		4 45		4 53	5 11		5 25		5 32	5 36			5
Muswell Hill „			3 26	3 41	3 46				4 51						5 31		5 38				5
Alxndra P. „			3 29	3 44	3 49				4 54						5 34		5 41				5
East End.... „	3 10					4 2		4 34			4 57		5 15				5 40				6
Finchley.... „	3 14					4 6		4 38			5 1		5 19				5 44				6
Torrugtn P. „	3 18					4 10		4 42			5 5		5 23				5 48				6
Totteridge „	3 22					4 14		4 46			5 9		5 27				5 52				6
H. Barnet ar	3 27					4 19		4 51			5 14		5 32				5 57				6
Mill Hill.... „	3 24					4 14				5 5						5 49				
Edgware.. arr	3 30					4 19				5 11						5 55				
Hornsey....				3 39		4 8		4 48					5 23	5 39			5 46		
Wood Grn 3 [Hatch				3 42		4 11		4 51				5 26	5 45			5 49		
Southgate & Colney				3 46		4 5	4 16		4 56				5 31	5 48			5 54		
Oakleigh Prk, Whet						4 11			5 2					5 52			6 0		
Barnet [stone						4 14			5 5				5 24	5 55			6 3		
Potter's Bar.						4 24							a	5 58				
Hatfield 126, 119.						4 36		4 53				5 42					
Welwyn....						4 46						5 50					
Stevenage....						4 58						6 1					
Hitchin 124, 209 ar 3 48					5 5		5 13			5 44	6 8					

Extra.—King's Cross (G.N.) to Holloway at 9 13 mrn. and 12 noon. Moorgate St. to King's Cross at 8 57, 9 9, 9 20, 12, 10 48, and 11 48 (Mondays only) mrn.; 12 5 and 10 10 aft. **Extra on Saturdays.**—Holloway to Alexandra Park and 2 32 aft., 1,2,3 class, stopping. Broad Street to Alexandra Park at 2 22 aft. 1,2,3 class, stopping. King's Cross to Ba at 1 25, 2 31, and 3 10 aft. **☞ For other Trains** between London and Wood Green, see page 118.

ALEXANDRA PALACE.—An additional Service between King's Cross and Alexandra Palace and Wood Green Stations on Special Fête Days.

ORNSEY, SOUTHGATE, BARNET, HATFIELD, and HITCHIN.—Great Northern.

&2	1&2	1&2	1&2	1,2,3	1&2	1&2	1&2	¶	1&2	1&2	1&2	1&2	1&2	1&2	non	1&2	1&2	1&2	1&2	1&2	1&2	1&2	1,2,3	1&2	1,2,3	1&2	1,2,3	1,2,3	1&2
gov	gov	gov	gov	mrn	gov	gov	gov		gov	gov	gov	gov	gov	gov	non	gov	gov	gov	gov	gov	gov	gov	aft	gov	aft	gov	aft	aft	gov
...	...	...	...	1035	...	...	...	1035	1055	...	...	...	12 0	12 0	...	1220	...	1235	...	1252	...	1 7	...	1 37	1 37	1 45	...		
...	...	...	...	1110	...	...	...	1170	1128	...	...	...	1235	1235	...	1253	...	1 10	...	1 26	...	1 41	...	2 12	2 12	2 19		
...	1040	...	...	...	1120	1120	1138	...	...	1225	1250	1250	...	...	1 18	...	1 37	1 49	1 58	2 5	...	2 14	2 27						
...	1042	...	...	...	1122	1122	1140	...	...	1227	1252	1252	...	...	1 20	...	1 39	1 51	2 0	2 7	...	2 16	2 29						
...	1044	...	1116	...	1124	1124	1142	...	...	1229	1254	1254	1257	...	1 22	...	1 41	1 53	2 2	9 2	16	2 18	2 31						
...	1048	...	1119	...	1128	1128	1146	...	...	1233	1258	1258	...	1 1	1 26	...	1 45	1 57	2 6	2 13	20	2 22	2 35						
...	1059	1110	1128	...	1140	1145	1155	...	...	1240	1 4	1 10	1 15	...	1 32	...	2 2	2 8	2 14	2 25	2 30	2 35	2 45						
...	11 3	...	1133	...	1145	...	12 0	...	...	1245	1 9	...	1 20	...	1 37	...	2 7	2 13	2 19	...	2 35	2 40							
.032	...	1057	...	1128	...	...	1148	1217	1227	...	...	1 7	...	1 17	1 52	...	...	1 7	...	...	...	2 47							
.035	...	11 0	...	1131	...	...	1151	1220	1230	...	...	1 10	...	1 20	1 55	...	...	...	...	...	2 50								
.037	...	11 2	...	1133	...	...	1152	1222	1232	...	...	1 12	...	1 22	1 57	...	...	...	...	2 52									
.039	...	11 5	...	1136	...	...	1155	1225	1235	...	...	1 15	...	1 24	2 0	...	...	...	...	2 55									
.042	...	11 8	...	1139	...	...	1159	1228	1238	...	...	1 18	...	1 27	2 3	...	...	...	...	2 58									
.050	11 6	1112	1118	1136	1143	1148	1153	12 4	12 4	1232	1242	1248	1 13	1 23	1 23	1 32	1 47	2 7	2 10	2 17	2 22	...	2 39	2 43	...	3 2		
.054	1110	1116	...	...	1147	1152	...	12 8	...	1236	1246	...	1 17	...	1 27	1 36	1 45	2 11	...	2 21	2 26	...	2 45	2 47					
.058	1114	1120	...	...	1151	1156	...	1212	...	1240	1250	...	1 21	...	1 31	1 40	1 49	2 15	...	2 25	2 30	...	2 49	2 51					
1 4	1119	1126	...	...	1157	...	...	1218	...	...	1256	...	1 27	...	...	1 46	1 55	2 21	...	2 31	...	...	2 55	...				
1 7	1122	1129	...	...	12 0	...	...	1221	...	...	1259	...	1 30	...	...	1 49	1 58	2 24	...	2 34	...	2 42	2 58	...				
...	...	...	...	...	12 0	...		1244	...	...	...	1 35	...	...	...	2 34	...	...	2 55									
...	...	...	...	...	12 4	...		1248	...	...	...	1 39	...	...	...	2 38	...	...	2 59									
...	...	...	...	...	12 8	...		1252	...	...	...	1 43	...	...	...	2 42	...	...	3 3									
...	...	...	...	...	1212	...		1256	...	...	...	1 47	...	...	...	2 46	...	...	3 7									
...	...	...	...	...	1217	...		1 1	...	...	...	1 51	...	...	...	2 51	...	...	3 12									
...	...	...	...	...	12 9	...			...	...	...	1 44	...	...	...	2 43	...											
...	...	...	...	...	1215	...			...	...	...	1 50	...	...	...	2 49	...											
...	...	...	1140	...	...	...		12 9	...	1252	...	1 28	...	...	2 16	...	...	...	3 7									
...	...	...	1143	...	...	...		1212	...	1255	...	1 31	...	...	2 19	...	...	...	3 13									
...	...	...	1148	...	...	...		1217	...	1 0	...	1 36	...	...	2 24	...	...	...	3 17									
...	...	...	1154	...	...	...		1223	...	1 6	...		...	...	2 30	...	...	...	3 22									
...	...	...	1157	...	...	...		1226	...	1 9	gov 1 29		...	...	2 33	...	...	...	3 26									
...	...	...	...	...	1210	...			...	...	1 39		...	...	2 43	...	...											
...	...	...	...	...	...	...			...	...	1 52		...	...	2 54	...	...		3 13									
...	...	...	...	...	...	...			...	...	2 1		...	...														
...	...	...	...	...	...	...			...	...	2 18		...	...														
...	...	...	1155	...	1230	...			...	...	2 20		...	...														

Note: the ¶ column carries the vertical note "A carriage detached at Hatfield." and the right-hand margin carries "Saturdays only." and "A carriage detached at Hatfield."

&2	1,2,3	1&2	1&2	1&2	1&2	1&2	1,2,3	1&2	1&2	1&2	1&2	1&2	1&2	1&2	1&2	1&2	1&2	1,2,3	1&2	1,2,3	1&2	1&2	1&2	1&2	1&2
gov	aft	gov	gov	gov	gov	gov	gov	gov	gov	gov	gov	gov	gov	gov	gov	aft	gov	aft	gov	aft	gov	gov	gov	gov	gov
...	5 35	5 35	5 35	46	...	...	5 53	...	5 53	6 39	6 55	6 55	...	7 25	...	7 25	8 0	8 0	...	8 53	8 53	9 43	9 43	1050	1050
...	5 38	5 39	5 58	6 22	...	...	6 28	...	6 28	7 12	7 30	7 30	...	8 0	...	8 8	8 32	8 33	8 33	9 27	9 27	1017	1017	1126	1126
...	5 48	5 55	6 9	6 ...	...	6 28	6 44	...	7 0	7 30	7 35	7 35	...	...	8 16	8 16	8 40	8 40	9 46	9 46	1044	1044	1138	1138		
...	5 50	5 57	6 11	6 11	...	6 30	6 46	...	7 2	7 10	7 37	7 37	...	...	8 18	8 18	8 42	8 44	9 48	9 48	1046	1046	1140	1140		
...	5 52	5 59	6 13	6 27	...	6 32	6 48	...	7 4	7 16	7 39	7 39	8 4	...	8 20	8 37	8 44	8 44	9 50	9 50	1048	1048	1142	1142		
...	5 56	6 3	6 17	6 31	...	6 36	6 52	...	7 8	7 20	7 43	7 43	8 8	...	8 24	8 41	8 48	8 48	9 54	9 54	1052	1052	1146	1146		
...	6 5	6 16	6 22	6 38	...	6 45	7 0	...	7 15	7 30	7 50	8 0	8 15	...	8 40	8 50	9 59	10	10 0	10 0	5 11	5 11	1155	12 0		
...	6 21	6 27	6 42	...	...	6 50	...	...	7 20	7 35	7 55	8 5	8 20	...	8 56	9 10	...	10 5	10 5	11 5	11 5	1110	12 0	12 5		
6 52	...	...	...	6 32	...	...	7 26	48	...	...	...	7 57	...	8 27	...	...	9 27	...							
6 55	...	...	...	6 35	...	...	7 56	51	...	...	...	8 0	...	8 30	...	...	9 30	...							
6 57	...	...	...	6 37	...	...	7 7	6 53	...	...	...	8 3	...	8 32	...	...	9 32	...							
6 0	...	...	...	6 40	...	...	7 10	6 53	...	...	...	8 5	...	8 34	...	...	9 35	...							
6 3	...	...	...	6 43	...	...	7 13	6 59	...	...	...	8 8	...	8 37	...	...	9 38	...							
6 8	6 12	6 25	6 30	6 48	6 48	6 54	7 8	7 18	7 8	7 23	7 38	7 58	8 8	8 13	8 23	8 42	8 48	9 9	9 13	9 19	9 43	10 8	1013	11 8	1113	12 3	12 8
6 12	...	6 29	6 34	...	6 52	6 58	7 4	...	7 22	...	7 27	...	8 2	...	8 17	8 27	8 46	...	9 17	...	...	1017	...	1117	12 7		
6 16	...	6 33	6 38	...	6 56	7 2	...	7 26	...	7 31	...	8 6	...	8 21	8 31	8 50	...	9 21	...	...	1021	...	1121	1211			
...	...	6 39	6 42	...	...	7 8	...	7 32	...	...	...	8 27	...	...	...	...	...	...							
...	...	6 42	...	...	...	7 11	...	7 35	...	...	...	8 30	...	...	...	...	...	...							
6 20	...	6 42	...	7 0	...	7 35	...	8 10	...	...	8 35	8 54	...	9 25	...	...	1025	...	1125	1215					
6 24	...	6 46	...	7 4	...	7 39	...	8 14	...	...	8 39	8 58	...	9 29	...	...	1029	...	1129	1219					
6 29	...	6 50	...	7 8	...	7 43	...	8 18	...	...	8 43	9 2	...	9 33	...	...	1033	...	1133	1223					
6 32	...	6 54	...	7 12	...	7 47	...	8 22	...	...	8 47	9 6	...	9 37	...	...	1037	...	1137	1227					
6 37	...	6 57	...	7 17	...	7 52	...	8 27	...	...	8 52	9 11	...	9 42	...	...	1042	...	1142	1232					
6 29	...	6 51	...	...	...	7 44	...	...	...	...	...	9 34	...	...	1033	...	1133	...							
6 35	...	6 57	...	...	...	7 50	...	...	...	...	...	9 40	...	...	1039	...	1139	...							
...	...	...	6 53	...	...	7 13	...	7 43	...	8 13	...	...	9 5	...	9 48	1013	...	1113	...	1215					
...	...	...	6 56	...	...	7 16	...	7 46	...	8 16	...	...	9 12	...	9 51	1016	...	1116	...	1218					
...	6 19	...	7 0	...	...	7 20	...	7 50	...	8 20	...	...	9 19	...	9 55	1019	...	1121	...	1223					
...	gov	...	7 6	...	gov	7 26	...	7 56	...	8 26	...	...	9 25	...	10 1	1027	...	1127	...	c					
...	6 26	...	7 9	...	7 20	7 29	...	8 0	...	8 29	...	...	9 28	...	10 4	1030	...	1130	...	1232					
...	6 36	...	...	...	7 30	...	...	...	...	...	...	9 38	...	...	1043	...	...	...	1243						
...	6 49	...	...	...	7 42	...	...	...	...	9 13	...	9 44	...	1052	...	...	...	1255							
...	7 0	...	...	...	7 50	...	...	...	...	...	...	9 53	...	...	...	...	...	...							
...	7 12	...	...	...	8 1	...	...	...	...	...	...	10 5	...	...	...	...	...	...							
...	7 18	...	...	...	...	...	...	...	...	9 34	...	9 34	...	...	...	...	...	...							

Note: the right-hand margin carries "Weds. & Fris." and the note "c".

∗∗∗ For **SUNDAY TRAINS**, see page 119.   ¶ Passengers not conveyed from King's Cross to Finsbury Park.
A carriage detached.   c Stop when required to take up, and set down on informing the Guard at the preceding Station.
Torrington Park, Woodside; 2, Totteridge and Whetstone: 3, Station for Alexandra Park.
☞ For **other Trains** between London and Wood Green, see page 118.

June 1876

FINSBURY PARK No.7 SIGNAL BOX

13.   Finsbury Park No.7 was the first signal box north of the junction with
the main line. This view, taken on 25th March 1966, shows blast walls in the
foreground erected for protection during World War II, and a ladder so that
signalmen could climb safely over the lineside cabling erected for the
proposed tube extension. (G.W. Goslin Collection)

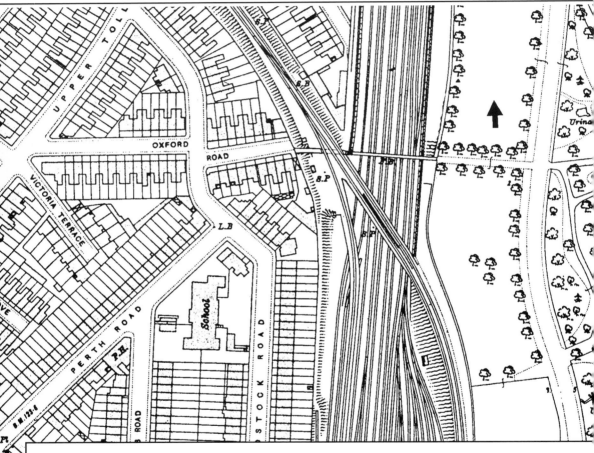

The area immediately north of Finsbury Park station in 1912, showing the line to Highgate and
Alexandra Palace diverging to the left. Down branch services ascended a gradient to the west of the
formation, whilst those travelling in the opposite direction were carried on a bridge over the
main line, and came in on the east side. The box (S.B.) stood a little beyond the junction, to
the north east of the formation.

14.   By the early 1970s, the box was disused and derelict. The down line from Finsbury
Park station is in the left foreground, whilst the up track continues on a straighter course
to the right. (I. Baker / Connor & Butler Collection)

STROUD GREEN

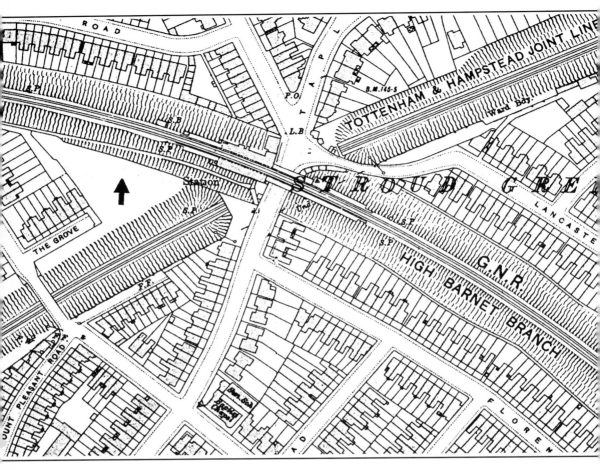

Stroud Green station was opened on 11th April 1881. It was erected on or near the site of an earlier signal box named 'Reservoir', and had its entrance in Stapleton Hall Road. It was constructed almost entirely of wood, and consisted of two side platforms, as indicated on the 1912 Ordnance Survey plan above. It occupied an elevated position, being partly on viaduct, and partly on embankment. Down below, deep in cutting, lay the Tottenham & Hampstead Joint Line, which linked the LTSR at Barking with Kentish Town, and Gospel Oak. According to surveys carried out by the Great Northern Railway, Stroud Green was the only station between Finsbury Park and Alexandra Palace to see an increase in bookings between 1914 and 1919, whereas all the others declined. However, passengers were eventually wooed away by other forms of transport, and the last four years of the 1920s saw the number of annual season ticket holders drop from 947 to 690. This was perhaps ironic, as more and more people were then moving into the area, as a result of larger houses being converted into flats, but these apparently preferred to use the buses and Underground for their journeys to and from work. If the proposed conversion of the route into part of the Northern Line had taken place, patronage would no doubt have returned, but by the time of closure in 1954, Stroud Green station was a sad deserted place, with the footsteps of the few remaining passengers echoing from the empty wooden platforms.

15. Here we look along Stapleton Hall Road in the early years of the twentieth century, and see the station entrance to the right. (Lens of Sutton)

16. The station master's house, seen to the right was in use as a hairdresser's shop in the mid-1930s. (LT Museum)

17. A class N2 0-6-2T brings an eight coach train, formed of two "Quad-Art" articulated sets into the station, en-route to Moorgate in the 1930s. Being articulated, the stock made economic use of bogies, as they only had five instead of eight as would have been the case with four individual coaches. (Lens of Sutton)

18. The freshly painted up side buildings are seen from a departing down train during the same decade. (Photomatic)

19. No.2663, another class N2 0-6-2T, drifts into the station with a two-car Finsbury Park - Alexandra Palace train on 11th August 1945. As part of the pre-war electrification scheme, the trackbed was raised at some stations so that tube trains could use the platforms, and conductor rails were laid on the down side. (H.C. Casserley)

20. On the same occasion, we take a general look at the station from the London end. A signal box once stood 4 chains to the west of the up platform, but this closed in 1932 following the introduction of multiple-aspect colour light signalling between Finsbury Park No.7 and Highgate. (H.C. Casserley)

G. N. R.	
9539 Series E	Series E 9539
STROUD GREEN to STROUD GREEN	
CROUCH END CROUCH END	
Fare 1d. Third Class Fare 1d.	
SEE CONDITIONS ON BACK	

G. N. R.	
0223 STROUD GREEN	STROUD GREEN 0223
HIGHBURY (TUBE ST'N) (TUBE STATION) HIGHBURY (TUBE)	
Available First Class to FINSBURY PARK & thence by TUBE	
Fare 3d Fare 3d	
SEE CONDITIONS ON BACK.	

21. A general view looking towards Finsbury Park in 1945, shows the staff crossing in use. This was a dangerous feature owing to the track curvature. (Stations UK)

22. Although the majority of buildings were located on the west side of Stapleton Hall Road, the up platform had an additional waiting shelter to the east for the early morning crowds. By 1945 however, the crowds had disappeared. (Stations UK)

23.   Ex-Great Central Railway class F2 2-4-2T No.5777, propels the two-car Alexandra Palace-Finsbury Park shuttle at Stroud Green in the late 1940s. The conductor rails on this section were removed in 1952 for use at the eastern end of the District Line. (Photomatic)

24.   We now look towards Finsbury Park in January 1966. Although the station had been closed for nearly twelve years, it was still remarkably intact. (J.E. Connor)

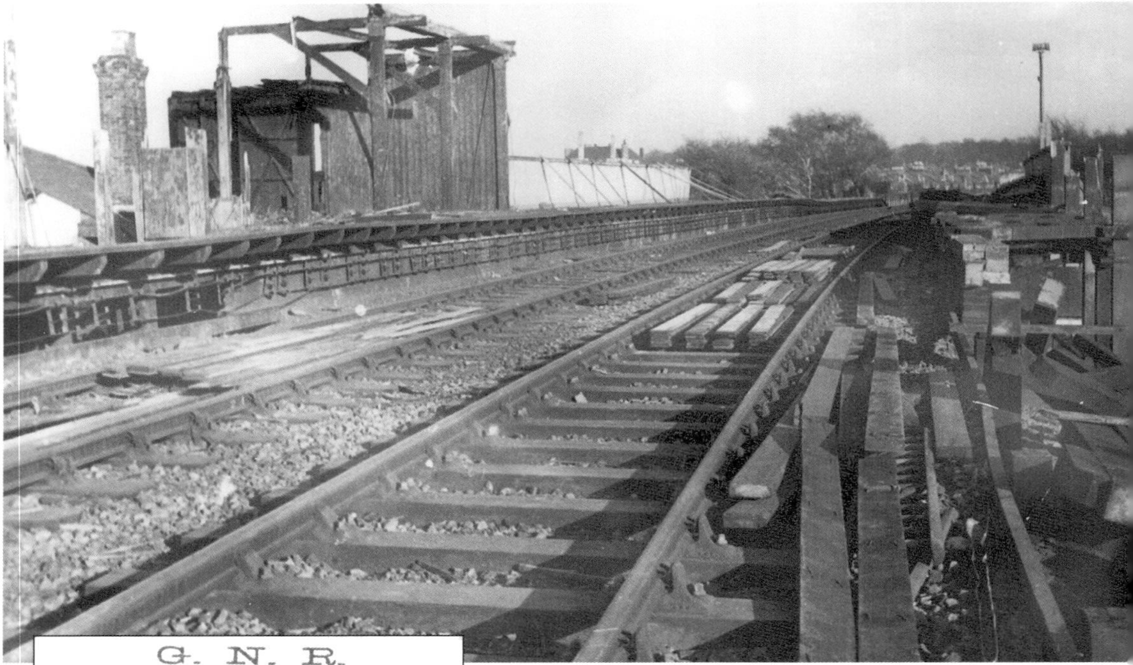

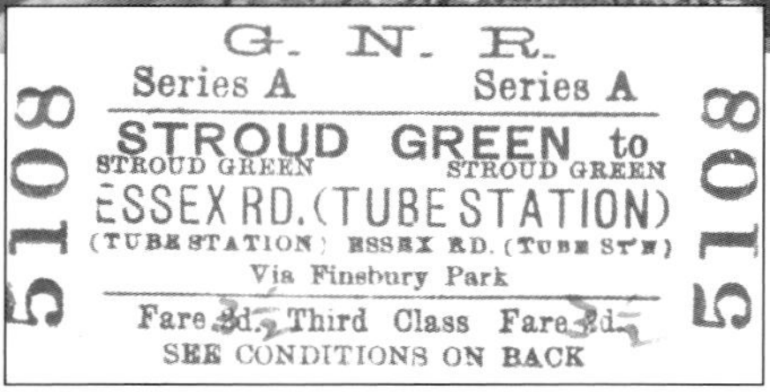

25. By 25th March 1966 only sections of platform and a fragment of the main up side building still remained, but even these were to vanish within days of being recorded by the photographer. (N.D. Mundy)

Week Days] ALEXANDRA PALACE BRANCH.—Great Northern.

Miles from London.	Station														
											Saturdays only.	Saturdays only.	Saturdays only.		Saturdays only.
	Victoria ....dep	6 20	8 18	8 26	9 15	9 49	1035	1058	1117	1158	1218	....	1 7	1 7	1 23
	Ludgate Hill.. "	7 19	8 50	9 6	9 50	1042	11 9	1131	1151	1232	1251	....	1 37	2 1	1 57
	Moorgate St... "	6 40	8 58	9 15	9 42	1050	....	1138	12 6	1240	1 9	1 20	1 48	1 56	2 6
	Aldersgate St. "	6 42	9 0	9 17	9 44	1052	....	1140	12 8	1242	1 11	1 22	1 50	1 58	2 8
	Farringdn St.. "	7 25	9 2	9 19	9 54	1054	1115	1142	1210	1244	1 13	1 24	1 52	2 6	2 10
	King's C. (Met.) "	7 29	9 6	9 23	9 58	1058	1119	1146	1214	1248	1 17	1 28	1 56	2 10	2 14
	" (Suburbn) "	7 32	9 9	9 26	....	11 1	1123	1149	1217	1251	1 22	1 32	1 59	2 13	2 17
	" (Main Ln. "	....	....	....	10 3	....	....	....	....	....	....	....	....	....	....
1½	Holloway	7 37	9 14	9 31	10 8	11 6	1128	1154	1222	1256	1 27	1 37	2 4	2 18	2 22
—	Broad St. dep	7 15	9 2	9 9	....	1032	1118	1142	....	Except Saturdays.	1 10	1 24	1 48	....	2 8
—	Shoreditch.. "	7 18	9 5	9 12	....	1035	1121	1145	....		1 13	1 27	1 51	....	2 11
—	Haggerston. "	7 20	9 7	9 14	....	1037	1123	1147	....		1 15	1 29	1 53	....	2 13
—	Dalston Jn.. "	7 25	9 10	9 16	....	1040	1125	1149	....		1 17	1 31	1 55	....	2 15
—	Mildmay Pk. "	7 27	9 12	9 18	....	1042	1127	1151	....		1 19	1 33	1 57	....	2 18
—	Canonbury.. "	7 29	9 14	9 20	....	1044	1129	1153	....		1 21	1 35	1 59	....	2 20
2½	Finsbury Park..	7 41	9 19	9 35	1011	11 9	1134	1158	1226	1 0	1 30	1 40	2 8	2 21	2 25
—	Stroud Green ..	7 44	9 22	9 38	1014	1112	1137	12 1	1229	1 3	1 33	1 43	2 11	2 24	2 28
3¾	Crouch End	7 46	9 24	9 40	1016	1114	1139	12 3	1231	1 5	1 35	1 45	2 13	2 26	2 30
4	Highgate	7 50	9 28	9 44	1020	1118	1143	12 7	1235	1 9	1 39	1 49	2 17	2 30	2 34
6	Muswell Hill....	7 54	9 32	9 48	1024	1122	1147	1211	1239	1 13	1 43	1 53	2 21	2 34	2 38
8	AlexandraPal. a	....	....	....	1027	1125	1150	1214	1242	1 16	1 46	1 56	2 24	2 37	2 41

Station															
		Saturdays only.	Saturdays only.												
Victoria ....dep	....	2 9	2 33	2 33	3 0	3 37	....	4 0	4 26	4 33	4 43	5 18	5 40	6 57	8 3
Ludgate Hill.. "	....	2 40	3 7	3 18	3 34	4 11	4 29	4 36	4 55	5 8	5 34	5 52	6 18	7 45	8 33
Moorgate St... "	....	2 50	3 13	3 29	3 49	4 3	4 18	4 46	5 1	5 18	5 29	6 2	6 28	7 33	8 21
Aldersgate St. "	....	2 52	3 15	3 31	3 51	4 5	4 20	4 48	5 3	5 20	5 31	6 4	6 30	7 35	8 23
Farringdn St.. "	....	2 54	3 17	3 33	3 53	4 17	4 34	4 50	5 5	5 22	5 38	6 6	6 32	7 49	8 37
King's C. (Met.) "	....	2 58	3 21	3 37	3 57	4 21	4 38	4 54	5 9	5 26	5 42	6 10	6 36	7 53	8 41
" (Suburbn) "	....	3 10	3 24	3 40	4 0	4 24	4 41	4 57	5 12	5 36	5 46	6 16	6 40	7 56	8 44
" (Main Ln. "	2 57	....	....	....	....	....	....	....	....	....	....	....	....	....	....
Holloway	3 2	3 15	3 29	3 45	4 5	4 29	4 46	5 2	5 17	5 41	5 51	6 21	6 45	8 1	8 49
Broad St. dep	2 47	2 58	3 13	3 40	....	4 3	4 23	4 39	5 2	5 22	5 33	6 8	6 28	7 39	8 37
Shoreditch.. "	2 50	3 1	3 16	3 43	....	4 6	4 26	4 42	5 5	5 24	5 36	6 6	6 31	7 42	8 40
Haggerston. "	2 52	3 3	3 18	3 45	....	4 8	4 28	4 44	5 7	5 27	5 38	6 8	6 33	7 44	8 42
Dalston Jn.. "	2 55	3 5	3 21	3 47	....	4 10	4 30	4 46	5 10	5 29	5 40	6 10	6 35	7 46	8 4[illegible]
Mildmay Pk. "	2 57	3 7	3 23	3 49	....	4 12	4 32	4 48	5 12	5 31	5 42	6 12	6 37	7 43	8 46
Canonbury.. "	2 59	3 9	3 25	3 51	....	4 14	4 34	4 50	5 14	5 33	5 44	6 14	6 39	7 50	8 48
Finsbury Park..	3 5	3 18	3 34	3 56	4 8	4 32	4 49	5 6	5 20	5 41	5 54	6 24	6 48	8 4	8 53
Stroud Green ..	3 8	3 21	3 37	3 59	4 11	4 35	4 52	5 9	5 23	5 47	5 57	6 27	6 51	8 7	8 56
Crouch End	3 10	3 23	3 39	4 1	4 13	4 37	4 54	5 11	5 25	5 49	5 59	6 29	6 53	8 9	8 58
Highgate	3 14	3 27	3 43	4 5	4 17	4 41	4 58	5 15	5 29	5 53	6 3	6 33	6 57	8 13	9 2
Muswell Hill....	3 18	3 31	3 47	4 9	4 21	4 45	5 2	5 19	5 33	5 57	6 7	6 37	7 1	8 17	9 6
AlexandraPal. a	3 21	3 34	3 50	4 12	4 24	4 48	5 5	5 22	5 36	6 0	6 10	6 40	7 4	8 20	9 9

☞ For Return Journey see opposite page

Mls	Fares.			Station														
																		Saturdays only.
				Alexandra Pal.	....	....	....	....	....	....	1042	1137	12 0	1257	2 3	3 2	3 7	3 24
[illegible]	....	....	....	Muswell Hill ..	8 12	8 45	8 54	9 15	9 47	1030	1045	1140	12 3	1 0	2 6	3 5	3 10	3 27
2¼	....	....	....	Highgate 138..	8 16	8 49	8 58	9 19	9 51	1034	1049	1144	12 7	1 4	2 10	3 9	3 14	3 31
3	....	....	....	Crouch End....	8 19	8 52	9 1	9 22	9 54	1037	1052	1147	1210	1 7	2 13	3 12	3 17	3 34
—	....	....	....	Stroud Green ..	8 21	8 54	9 3	9 24	9 56	1039	1054	1149	1212	1 9	2 15	3 14	3 19	3 36
4¼	....	....	....	Finsbury P. 146	8 25	8 58	9 7	9 28	10 0	1042	1058	1153	1216	1 13	2 19	3 18	3 23	3 40
—	....	....	....	Canonbury ar	8 34	9 2	9 11	9 35	10 4	1051	1111	12 8	1220	1 17	Except Saturdays.	3 22	....	3 45
—	....	....	....	Mildmay Pk. "	8 36	9 4	9 13	9 40	10 6	1053	1113	1210	1222	1 19		3 24	....	3 48
—	....	....	....	Dalston Junc. "	8 38	9 6	9 15	9 42	10 8	1055	1116	1212	1224	1 21		3 26	....	3 51
—	....	....	....	Haggerston . "	....	9 8	....	....	1010	1058	1118	1214	1226	1 23		3 28	....	3 53
—	....	....	....	Shoreditch.. "	....	9 10	....	....	1012	11 0	1121	1216	1228	1 26		3 31	....	3 56
—	....	....	....	Broad St. .. "	8 42	9 12	9 20	9 47	1015	11 3	1123	1219	1230	1 28		3 34	....	3 58
5½	....	....	....	Holloway	8 30	9 2	9 12	9 32	10 5	1047	11 3	1157	....	1 31	2 24	Saturdays only.	3 28	3 48
—	....	....	....	King's C (Y.R.) d	8 40	9 16	9 26	9 36	1011	1059	11 9	12 2	....	1 39	2 29		3 33	3 53
6½	....	....	....	" (Ter.) arr	8 34	9 6	9 17	....	....	1052	....	....	....	....	....		....	....
—	....	....	....	" (Met.) "	8 43	9 19	9 29	9 39	1014	11 2	1112	12 5	....	1 42	2 32		3 36	3 56
—	....	....	....	Farringdon St "	8 47	9 23	9 33	9 43	1018	11 6	1116	12 9	....	1 46	2 36		3 40	4 0
—	....	....	....	Aldersgate St. "	8 49	9 25	9 35	9 54	1020	11 8	1127	1211	....	1 48	2 38		3 49	4 2
—	....	....	....	Moorgate St. "	8 51	9 27	9 37	9 56	1022	1110	1129	1213	....	1 50	2 40		3 51	4 4
—	....	....	....	Ludgate Hill.. "	9 2	9 35	....	9 48	1039	1122	1122	1223	....	1 59	2 45		3 45	4 33
—	....	....	....	Victoria...... "	....	1011	....	1040	11 7	1157	1137	1258	....	2 41	3 20		4 42	5 1

Station															
Alexandra Pal.	3 47	4 40	4 44	5 17	5 43	5 47	5 50	6 35	7 1	7 9	7 33	8 30	9 17	....	....
Muswell Hill ..	3 50	4 43	4 47	5 20	5 46	5 50	5 53	6 38	7 4	7 12	7 36	8 32	9 20	....	....
Highgate 138..	3 54	4 47	4 51	5 24	5 50	5 54	5 57	6 42	7 8	7 16	7 40	8 36	9 24	....	....
Crouch End....	3 57	4 50	4 54	5 27	5 53	5 57	6 0	6 45	7 11	7 19	7 43	8 39	9 27	....	....
Stroud Green ..	3 59	4 52	4 56	5 29	5 55	5 59	6 2	6 47	7 13	7 21	7 45	8 41	9 29	....	....
Finsbury P. 146	4 3	4 56	5 0	5 33	5 59	6 3	6 6	6 51	7 18	7 25	7 49	8 45	9 35	....	....
Canonbury ar	4 15	....	5 4	5 42	6 4	....	....	6 56	7 26	7 33	7 57	9 13	9 47	....	....
Mildmay Pk. "	4 17	....	5 6	5 44	6 6	....	....	6 58	7 28	7 35	7 59	9 15	9 49	....	....
Dalston Junc. "	4 20	....	5 8	5 46	6 8	....	....	7 1	7 31	7 37	8 1	9 17	9 51	....	....
Haggerston . "	4 23	....	5 10	5 48	6 10	....	....	7 3	7 34	7 39	8 3	9 19	9 53	....	....
Shoreditch.. "	4 26	....	5 12	5 51	6 12	....	....	7 6	7 36	7 41	8 6	9 21	9 55	....	....
Broad St. .. "	4 28	....	5 15	5 53	6 15	....	....	7 9	7 38	7 44	8 8	9 24	9 58	....	....
Holloway	4 9	5 3	5 15	5 38	....	6 8	6 11	6 57	7 23	7 30	7 54	8 50	9 39	....	....
King's C (Y.R.) d	4 14	5 10	5 22	5 44	....	6 12	6 19	7 4	7 28	7 35	8 0	8 56	9 53	....	....
" (Ter.) arr	....	....	....	....	....	....	....	....	....	....	....	....	9 45	....	....
" (Met.) "	4 17	5 13	5 25	5 47	....	6 15	6 22	7 7	7 31	7 38	8 3	8 59	9 56	....	....
Farringdon St "	4 21	5 17	5 29	5 51	....	6 19	6 26	7 11	7 35	7 42	8 7	9 3	10 0	....	....
Aldersgate St. "	4 23	5 19	5 31	6 1	....	....	6 28	7 13	7 37	7 47	8 9	9 28	10 2	....	....
Moorgate St. "	4 25	5 21	5 33	6 3	....	....	6 30	7 15	7 39	7 49	8 11	9 30	10 4	....	....
Ludgate Hill.. "	4 36	5 31	5 41	5 57	....	6 26	....	7 57	....	7 48	8 20	9 9	1024	....	....
Victoria...... "	5 12	....	6 10	6 33	....	7 11	....	8 33	....	8 43	8 56	1022	....	....	....

September 1885

WEST OF STROUD GREEN

26.   Former GCR class F2 2-4-2T No.7111 commences the 1-in-72 climb towards Crouch End, soon after leaving Stroud Green on 6th June 1950. (D.A. Dant)

27.   Class C2 4-4-2T (later class C12) No.1505 approaches Crouch End station in pre-grouping days, having just passed beneath the road bridge carrying Crouch Hill. (Lens of Sutton)

28.   A North London Railway Broad Street-High Barnet train pounds up the gradient towards Crouch End on a winter's day in the early twentieth century, headed by 4-4-0T No.86. These services linking the NLR with the GNR Northern Heights lines were always worked by North London locomotives and stock, as the London & North Western Railway, who had a part-share in Broad Street, objected to Great Northern trains infiltrating their territory. (Lens of Sutton)

29.   Stirling 0-4-4WT No.248 approaches Crouch End with a GNR train for High Barnet during the same period. These locomotives were once a familiar sight on the Northern Heights. (Lens of Sutton)

30.	As part of the pre-war electrification scheme, a sub-station was erected to the west of the bridge carrying Crouch Hill over the line. Although the outer fabric was completed, it was never fitted-out internally, and of course remained unused. Here, work-stained class N2 0-6-2T No. 69593 makes a smoky ascent of the gradient with a freight train in January 1961, and passes the unfinished sub-station on the right. (D.I.D. Loveday/The Gresley Society)

31.	A view from beneath Crouch Hill bridge, looking towards Highgate in 1984, features the sub-station, now used as a community centre. (J.E. Connor)

CROUCH END

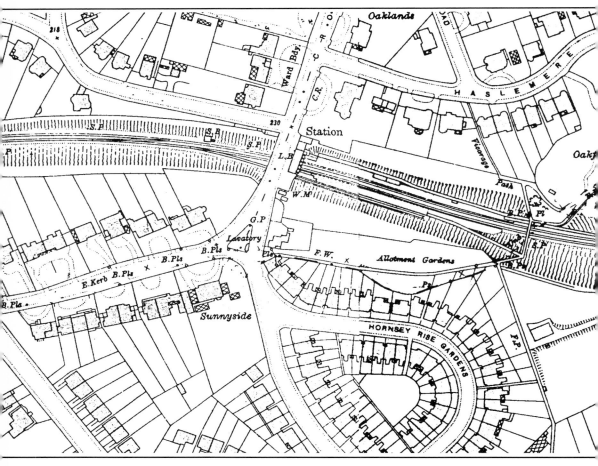

The station opened with the Finsbury Park - Edgware branch on 22nd August 1867, and was located to the east of the road bridge carrying Crouch End Hill. It had two side platforms, and was provided with a siding for coal traffic on the down side. To reach this, trains from Finsbury Park had to pass through the station, then reverse. These movements were controlled by a signal box, marked 'S.B', which like Stroud Green was closed following the installation of colour light signalling in 1932. The chief means

by which passengers entered or left the station was through the street level building on Crouch End Hill, although there was also a network of footpaths at the opposite end, which provided access to both platforms. The one on the up side was presumably for season ticket holders only, whilst the other seems to have been intended solely as an exit. The various pathways also included a pedestrian bridge, which crossed the line just east of the platform ends, and is clearly shown on the 1912 OS plan above.

32.   The street level building is viewed from the south side in about 1935, with a period telephone box in the foreground. (LT Museum)

33.   Here we look along the platforms towards Highgate in pre-grouping days. The awning on the down side was later lengthened. (Lens of Sutton)

34.   GNR 0-4-2 No.104 pauses at Crouch End with an up train around the turn of the century. Tender locomotives were not a frequent sight on Northern Heights passenger turns. (Lens of Sutton)

35.   Once again, we look along the platforms towards Highgate, but this time see them as they appeared in the 1930s. Comparison with the view on the previous page shows the extent by which the down side canopy had been lengthened. (Lens of Sutton)

36.   Ex-GNR class C12 4-4-2T No.7374 departs from Crouch End after World War II, with the two-car Finsbury Park to Alexandra Palace push-pull set. Cable runs for the unfinished electrification scheme can be seen alongside the up line. (P. Ransome-Wallis)

37.   The same loco, but now carrying the BR number 67374 arrives at the station in the early 1950s with a Finsbury Park-Alexandra Palace push-pull service, prior to the unused down side conductor rails being lifted. (Stations UK)

38.   Ex-GCR class F2 2-4-2T No.7107 departs with a Finsbury Park - Alexandra Palace train just prior to nationalisation. The loco was renumbered 67107 in September 1948, and scrapped in February 1949. (Real Photographs Co. Ltd.)

39.   Crouch End was the only station between Finsbury Park and Alexandra Palace to have received BR 'totem' style nameboards. It has been rumoured that Stroud Green was also provided with them, but photographic evidence suggests otherwise. This is the up platform on 22nd June 1954, with a totem clearly visible to the left. (R.M. Casserley)

40.　On 21st March 1959, the Railway Correspondence & Travel Society operated a special train over the Northern Heights behind class N2/1 0-6-2T No.69504. The down working is seen just west of Crouch End station. As to why the loco is carrying an upside down Hatfield destination board is anyone's guess! (Real Photographs Co. Ltd.)

41.　The return trip passes through the abandoned platforms. The pathway which once served the season ticket holders entrance can be seen between the two fences on the up side. (E. R. Wethersett)

42.   After closure to passenger traffic the route was retained for freight and transferring LT stock between Highgate depot and the Northern City Line. Here class N2/4 0-6-2T No.69568 blasts through Crouch End with a coal train in January 1961. (D.I.D. Loveday/The Gresley Society)

43.   Demolition of the platform buildings is in progress on 25th March 1966. (N.D. Mundy)

44. A train of 1938 Tube Stock passes through Crouch End on 12th June 1968, hauled by a London Transport battery locomotive. Platform alterations carried out in connection with the pre-war New Works Scheme can be clearly seen on both sides. (Kenneth Harris)

45. The abandoned platforms were photographed looking east in 1984. The trackbed is now in use as 'The Parkland Walk'. (J.E. Connor)

HIGHGATE

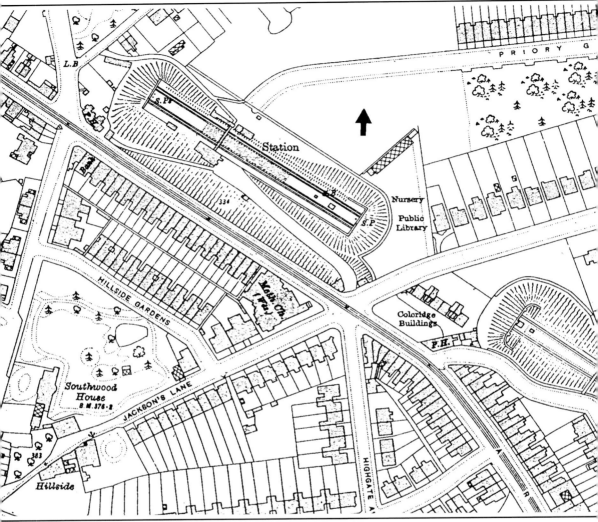

Highgate was one of the original stations on the Edgware Highgate & London Railway, and opened with the line in 1867. It was located deep in cutting, and was sandwiched between two tunnels. Prior to 1932 it had a signal box near its eastern end, but like those already mentioned at Stroud Green and Crouch End, this closed as a result of re-signalling. At the same time, an intermediate box between Crouch End and Highgate, which was known as Archway, was also closed and subsequently demolished. This was located west of the bridge over Stanhope Road, and stood on the down side of the line.

46. Highgate East Tunnel was located at the London end of the station, and had a length of 139 yards. The twin tunnel mouths are seen in 1969, with both tracks still in position, and London Transport line-side cabling adjoining the up side. (J.E. Connor)

47. We now look towards the tunnel mouths in the 1990s, and see them surrounded with lush vegetation. This is where the Parkland Walk from Finsbury Park finishes, and there is no public access to either bore. (J.E. Connor)

48.   Highgate station was initially provided with two side platforms and as certain trains were expected to terminate there, it had a centre road for use as a run-round loop.(Commercial postcard / Author's Collection)

49.   The arrangement lasted until the early 1880s, when the loop was lifted, and replaced by a new island, which rendered the earlier platforms redundant. (Commercial Postcard / Author's Collection)

50. The station was photographed from the London end around the turn of the century, with a cast-iron gent's urinal in the foreground. (Commercial Postcard/Author's Collection)

51. The original street level building was located at the bottom of an approach leading from the north-west side of Shepherd Road. Although a new booking office was later constructed on the footbridge, the structure seen here survived into the late 1930s. (Lens of Sutton)

5422

G. N. R.
Series E   Series E
HIGHGATE   to
HIGHGATE   HIGHGATE
STROUD GREEN
STROUD GREEN   STROUD GREEN
Fare 1½d.   Third Class   Fare 1½d.
SEE CONDITIONS ON BACK

5422

52.   LMSR class 3F 0-6-0T No.7517 of Devons Road shed emerges from Highgate East Tunnel with a Broad Street-High Barnet train on 5th June 1937. (H.C. Casserley)

53.   Here we look along the platforms towards Finsbury Park in the 1930s. The structure adjoining the footbridge accommodated the ticket office, and was added as an afterthought to provide better booking facilities for passengers entering the premises from either side. (Lens of Sutton)

54.   Further rebuilding came in the wake of the pre-war New Works Plan, when the station was earmarked for a complete facelift. The island platform was to be retained, but all GNR buildings would be replaced by smart, modern structures, typical of those favoured by the London Passenger Transport Board. The Archway Road entrance, designed by Charles Holden, was to be an impressive affair, complete with decorative weathervane featuring Dick Whittington and his cat. A sub-surface booking hall was to be provided below the existing island platform, and linked to it by a short flight of stairs. Nearby, escalators were planned to provide access to a new tube station, located sixty feet beneath the surface. When the Underground extension from Archway to East Finchley was opened on 3rd July 1939, the low level platforms at Highgate were still not ready, so trains had to pass through without stopping. Following the outbreak of hostilities, these platforms were pressed into use as air-raid shelters and trains began to call for the convenience of shelterers after September 1940. A few months later, on 19th January 1941, a full public service commenced operation, and the new Highgate tube station was officially opened. All work on the LNER premises eventually ceased due to wartime conditions and was never resumed. This is the view looking towards Alexandra Palace, with LT roundels in position, ready for the tube trains which never came. A new platform building erected in 1940/1 is partially hidden behind a surviving section of GNR structure. (Photomatic)

L.N.E.R in conjunction with
The LOCAL AUTHORITY

Admit one Person for Shelter
(if available) at

HIGHGATE Station

Persons permitted to use this Station as, or as a means of access to, an Air Raid Shelter do so at their own risk in all respects,
FOR FURTHER CONDITIONS SEE BACK

3rd Cl LNER
CIVIL DEFENCE
& HOME GUARD
SPECIAL DUTY TICKET
Issued subject to the Bye-laws, Regulations, Notices & Conditions published in the Co's Bills & Notices Available day of issue or following day or Satur-day to Monday.
Any Station on back
to HIGHGATE
Not Transferable
C   Fare 6d

3rd Cl LNER
CIVIL DEFENCE
& HOME GUARD
SPECIAL DUTY TICKET
issued subject to the Bye-laws, Regulations, Notices and Conditions published in the Co's Bills & Notices Available day of issue only
Highgate
To
Any Station on back
Not Transferable
C   Fare 6d

55.   On the last day at Highgate, we see enthusiasts on the platform and an up freight passing through, hauled by a class N2 0-6-2T. (Alan A. Jackson)

56.   After closure, the remnant of GNR island platform building shown in the previous picture was removed, leaving just that which was erected during 1940-1. For many years, 1954 posters still stuck stubbornly to its walls, and lighter patches of brickwork revealed where LT roundels had once been fixed. This is a view from the up side around 1969. The track was removed early in 1972. (I. Baker / Connor & Butler Collection)

57.   When the station was rebuilt in the early years of the World War II, very little of the earlier premises were left standing. This building, standing on the long-disused up platform was one of the few exceptions however, and still survives as a private house. The view dates from 1967. (J.E. Connor)

58.   The 332yd Highgate West Tunnel is seen here on 24th June 1954. The conductor rails on this section were energised, as the track was used as a headshunt by tube trains entering or leaving Highgate Wood Sidings. (H.C. Casserley)

LONDON, HIGHGATE, and MUSWELL HILL.—Great Northern.

Down.	mrn	mrn	mrn	mrn	mrn	mrn	mrn	mrn	aft (Saturdays only.)	aft	aft	aft	aft	aft	aft	aft	aft	aft (Saturdays only.)	aft	aft	aft	aft	aft	aft	aft (Except Saturdays.)	aft	aft	aft	aft	aft	aft	aft
Victoria ....dep.	6 46	....	8 3	8 13	8 40	9 48	1038	1156	1221	....	1e3	1 3	1e39	....	1e55	2e7	2 33	2 48	3 3	3 36	4 23	4 33	4 48	5 21	5 38	5 45	6 3	6 38	6 45	8 3	8 20	1040
Ludgate Hill .... "	7 21	....	8 32	8 48	9 14	1035	1126	1231	1258	1 4	1e35	2 0	2e12	....	2e27	2e40	3 6	3 22	3 36	4 22	4 56	5 6	5 31	5 54	6 6	6 19	6 39	7 10	7 20	8 33	9 26	1112
Moorgate Street "	7 10	....	8 40	8 58	9 22	1050	1120	1240	1 8	1 19	1e45	1 56	2e15	2e27	2e44	2e50	3 13	3 29	3 50	4 17	5 1	5 19	5 31	6 1	6 17	6 28	7 0	7 8	7 36	8 21	9 15	1119
Farringdon St. "	7 27	....	8 44	9 2	9 26	1054	1131	1244	1 12	1 23	1e49	2 6	2e19	2e31	2e48	2e54	3 17	3 33	3 54	4 27	5 5	5 23	5 38	6 5	6 21	6 32	7 4	7 17	7 40	8 37	9 32	1123
King's Cross (Met) "	7 31	....	8 48	9 6	9 30	1058	1135	1248	1 16	1 27	1e53	2 10	2e23	2e35	2e52	2e58	3 21	3 37	3 58	4 31	5 9	5 27	5 42	6 9	6 25	6 36	7 8	7 21	7 44	8 41	9 36	1127
" (Suburban) "	7 34	....	8 51	9 9	9 33	11 1	1138	1251	1 20	1 30	1e56	2 13	2e27	2¼be	2e55	3e8	3 30	3b45	4 1	4 35	5 12	5 35	5 45	6 13	6 28	6 40	7 11	7b30	7 47	8 46	9 39	1145
Holloway	7 39	....	8 56	9 14	9 38	11 6	1143	1256	1 25	1 35	2e1	2 18	2e32	2e53	3e0	3e13	3 35	3 45	4 6	4 40	5 17	5 40	5 50	6 18	6 31	6 45	7 16	7g38	7 52	8 51	9 44	1150
Broad Street dep.	7 15	7 57	8 39	9 2	9 11	1032	1128	1222	1 10	Except Saturdays.	1e48	2e2	2e17	2e27	2e47	2e55	3e18	3 40	3c40	4 18	5 2	5 24	5 33	6 3	6 20	6 27	6c55	7 24	7 40	8 37	9 18	1055
Shoreditch .... "	7 17	....	8 41	9 4	....	1034	1130	1224	1 2		1e50	2e4	2e19	2e29	2e49	2e47	3e20	3 32	3c42	4 20	5 4	5 17	5 35	6 5	6 17	6 29	6c47	7 17	7 32	8 39	9 20	1057
Haggerston .... "	7 20	....	8 44	9 7	....	1037	1133	1227	1 5		1e53	2e7	2e22	2e32	2e52	2e50	3e23	3 35	3c45	4 23	5 7	5 20	5 38	6 8	6 20	6 32	6c50	7 20	7 35	8 42	9 23	11 0
Dalston Junc.. "	7 25	8 3	8 46	9 9	9 16	1039	1135	1229	1 15		1e55	2e9	2e24	2e34	2e54	3e0	3e25	3 45	3c47	4 25	5 9	5 29	5 40	6 10	6 25	6 34	7c0	7 29	7 45	8 44	9 25	11 2
Mildmay Park "	7 27	8 5	8 48	9 11	9 18	1041	1137	1231	1 17		1e57	2e11	2e26	2e36	2e56	3e2	3e27	3 47	3c49	4 27	5 11	5 31	5 42	6 12	6 27	6 36	7c2	7 31	7 47	8 46	9 27	11 4
Canonbury .... "	7 29	8 7	8 50	9 13	9 20	1043	1139	1233	1 19		1e59	2e13	2e28	2e38	2e58	3e4	3e29	3 49	3c51	4 29	5 13	5 33	5 44	6 14	6 29	6 38	7c4	7 33	7 49	8 48	9 29	11 6
Finsbury Park......	7 43	8 15	9 3	9 19	9 41	11 9	1147	1 0	1 28	1 41	2e4	2 21	2e35	2e56	3e4	3e16	3 38	3 56	4 9	4 44	5 20	5 43	5 53	6 22	6 36	6 48	7 19	7 41	7 55	8 55	9 48	1153
Stroud Green	7 46	....	....	9 22	9 44	1112	1150	1 3	1 31	1 44	2e7	2 24	2e38	2e59	3e7	3e19	3 41	3 59	4 12	4 47	5 23	5 46	5 56	6 25	6 39	6 51	7 22	7 44	7 58	8 58	9 51	1156
Crouch End........	7 48	....	....	9 24	9 46	1114	1152	1 5	1 33	1 46	2e9	2 26	2e40	3e1	3e9	3e21	3 43	4 1	4 14	4 49	5 25	5 48	5 58	6 27	6 41	6 53	7 24	7 46	8 0	9 0	9 53	1158
Highgate	7 52	8 25	....	9 28	9 50	1118	1156	1 9	1 37	1 50	2e13	2 30	2e44	3e5	3e13	3e25	3 47	4 5	4 18	4 53	5 29	5 52	6 2	6 31	6 45	6 57	7 28	7 50	8 4	9 4	9 57	12 2
Muswell Hill ..arr.	7 56	8 29	9 13	9 32	9 54	1122	12 0	1 13	1 41	1 54	2e17	2 34	2e48	3e9	3e17	3e29	3 51	4 9	4 22	4 57	5 33	5 56	6 6	6 35	6 49	7 1	7 32	7 54	8 8	9 8	10 1	12 6

Up.	mrn	mrn	mrn	mrn	mrn	mrn	mrn	mrn	mrn	mrn	mrn	mrn	aft	aft	aft	aft	aft (Saturdays only.)	aft	aft (Saturdays only.)	aft	aft	aft	aft	aft	aft	aft	aft	aft	aft	aft	aft	aft	aft	aft
Muswell Hill ..dep.	8 2	812	821	829	8 45	9 1	9 14	9 17	9 28	9 47	1030	1137	1 0	1 45	2c10	2e14	3 3	3 10	350	4 27	447	4e55	5 48	6 32	6 38	7 0	7 10	7c20	7 36	8 15	8 29	9 23	1030	1215
Highgate 203......	8 6	816	825	833	8 49	9 5	9 18	9 21	9 32	9 51	1034	1141	1 4	1 49	2c14	2e18	3 7	3 14	354	4 31	451	4e59	5 52	6 36	6 42	7 4	7 14	7c24	7 40	8 19	8 33	9 27	1034	1219
Crouch End........	8 9	819	828	836	8 52	9 8	9 21	9 24	9 35	9 54	1037	1144	1 7	1 52	2c17	2e21	310	3 17	357	4 34	454	5e2	5 55	6 39	6 45	7 7	7 17	7c27	7 43	8 22	8 36	9 30	1037	1222
Stroud Green	811	821	830	838	8 54	9 10	9 23	9 26	9 37	9 56	1039	1146	1 9	1 54	2c19	2e23	312	3 19	359	4 36	456	5e4	5 57	6 41	6 47	7 9	7 19	7c29	7 45	8 24	8 38	9 32	1039	1224
Finsbury Park 212	815	824	833	841	8 58	9 13	9 26	9 30	9 42	10 0	1042	1154	1 13	1 56	2 22	2e27	317	3 23	4 3	4 40	5 0	5e8	6 1	6 45	6 52	713	7 22	7c33	7 49	8 28	8 42	9 36	1044	1227
Canonbury ..arr.	823	828	837	...	9 2	9 18	....	....	9 46	10 4	1052	1213	1 17	....	....	2e31	322	3c42	414	4e57	5 4	5e12	6c8	6 49	7 4	717	7 33	7c37	7c53	8 32	8 53	9 52	11 7	Mon., Wed., and Sats.
Mildmay Park "	825	830	839	...	9 4	9 20	....	....	9 48	10 6	1054	1215	1 19	....	....	2e33	324	3c44	416	4e59	5 6	5e14	6c11	6 51	7 6	719	7 35	7c39	7c55	8 34	8 55	9 54	11 9	
Dalston Junc.. "	827	833	841	850	9 6	9 22	....	9 35	9 51	10 8	1056	1217	1 21	....	....	2e36	326	3c46	418	5e1	5 8	5e16	6c13	6 54	7 8	721	7 37	7c41	7c57	8 36	8 57	9 56	1111	
Haggerston .... "	...	...	...	...	....	....	....	....	9 53	1010	1059	1219	1 23	....	....	2e38	328	3c48	420	5e3	510	5e18	6c16	6 56	7 10	723	7 39	7c44	7c59	8 38	8 59	9 58	1113	
Shoreditch .... "	...	...	...	...	....	....	....	....	9 55	1012	11 1	1221	1 25	....	....	2e40	331	3c50	422	5e5	512	5e20	6c18	6 58	7 12	725	7 41	7c46	8c1	8 40	9 1	10 0	1115	
Broad Street.. "	832	838	848	855	9 13	9 27	....	9 43	9 58	1015	11 4	1224	1 28	....	....	2e43	334	3c53	425	5e8	515	5e23	6c21	7 1	7 15	728	7 44	7c50	8c4	8 43	9 4	10 3	1118	
Holloway...........	818	828	...	844	9 1	9 21	9 31	9 40	9 50	10 5	1047	1159	1 22	2e3	2 27	2e39	322	3 28	4 9	4 45	5 5	5e17	6 6	c Saturdays only.	6 57	719	7 27	7c47	7 54	8 38	8 47	9 41	1049	1231
King's Cross (YR) ar	831	840	...	857	9 16	9 26	9 36	9 45	9 55	1011	1059	12 5	1 27	2e9	2 32	2e44	329	3 33	414	4 52	512	5e22	6 12		7 4	728	7 35	7c56	8 0	8 43	8 53	9 46	1054	....
" (Ter.) "	822	832	...	848	9 5	9 22	....	9 37	9 48	1025	1052	....	....	....	....	....	...	3 35	419	....	512	....	....		....	720	....	7c48	....	....	....	....	....	1236
" (Met.) "	834	843	...	9 0	9 19	9 29	9 39	9 48	9 58	1014	11 2	12 8	1 30	2e12	2 35	2e47	332	3 36	417	4 55	515	5e25	6 15		7 7	731	7 38	7c59	8 3	8 46	8 56	9 49	1057	....
Farringdon St... "	838	847	...	9 4	9 23	9 33	9 43	9 52	10 2	1018	11 6	1212	1 34	2e16	2 39	2e51	336	3 40	421	4 59	519	5e29	6 19		7 11	735	7 42	8c3	8 7	8 50	9 0	9 53	11 1	....
Moorgate Street "	842	851	...	9 8	9 27	9 37	....	9 56	10 6	1022	1110	1216	1 38	2e20	....	2e35	340	3 52	425	5 3	523	5e33	6 30		7 15	739	7 49	....	8 11	8 54	9 4	1019	1124	....
Ludgate Hill .... "	854	9 2	...	920	9 35	....	9 48	10 7	1010	1032	1122	1223	1 42	2e29	2 45	3e5	348	3 45	436	5 11	533	5e41	6 27		7 22	747	7 49	8c8	8 31	9 2	9 9	9 58	11 6	....
Victoria .... "	930	946	...	...	1011	1028	....	....	1043	11 7	1158	1258	2 18	....	3 21	3e38	424	4 48	512	5 40	610	6e10	7 11		8 0	822	8 33	8c44	9 4	9 37	9 42	1031	1216	....

b Depart from King's Cross Main Line Platform. c Except Saturdays. g Leaves at 7 30 aft. on Saturdays.

August 1893

LONDON, FINSBURY PARK, HIGHGATE, ALEXANDRA PALACE, EDGWARE, and HIGH BARNET.—Great Northern.

Week Days.

Miles from King's Cross.	Down.	mrn	mrn	mrn	mrn	mrn	mrn	mrn	mrn	mrn	mrn	mrn	mrn	mrn	mrn	mrn	mrn	mrn	mrn	mrn	mrn	mrn	mrn	mrn	mrn	mrn	mrn	mrn	mrn	mrn	mrn	mrn	mrn
	Moorgate Street.dep.	....	....	6 0	6 23	6 51	6 58	7 10	7 21	....	7 40	....	8 5	....	8 23	8 30	....	....	8 40	8 45	8 51	8 57	9 2	9 7	9 15	9 34	9 53	1010	1016	1024	1050	....	1116
	Aldersgate Street....	....	....	6 2	6 25	6 53	7 0	7 12	7 23	....	7 42	....	8 7	....	8 25	8 32	....	....	8 42	8 47	8 53	8 59	9 4	9 9	9 17	9 36	9 55	1012	1018	1026	1052	....	1118
	Farringdon Street....	....	....	6 4	6 27	6 55	7 2	7 14	7 25	....	7 44	....	8 9	....	8 27	8 34	....	....	8 44	8 49	8 55	9 1	9 6	9 11	9 19	9 38	9 57	1014	1020	1028	1054	....	1120
	King's Cross (Met.)*..	....	....	6 8	6 31	6 59	7 6	7 18	7 29	....	7 48	....	8 13	....	8 31	8 38	....	....	8 48	8 53	8 59	9 5	9 10	9 15	9 23	9 42	10 1	1018	1024	1032	1058	....	1124
	" (Suburban) ...	5a22	5a30	6 15	6a40	7 2	7 9	7 21	7 33	....	7 51	....	8 16	....	8 34	8 41	8b45	....	8 51	8 57	9 2	9 8	9 13	9 18	9 30	9 45	10 5	1021	1027	1035	11 1	11a9	1127
1¼	Holloway †	5 27	5 35	6 20	6 44	7 8	....	....	7 38	....	7 56	....	8 23	....	8 39	8 46	....	....	8 56	9 1	9 6	9 13	9 17	9 23	9 35	9 50	1010	1026	1032	1040	11 5	1114	1132
—	Broad Street ¶ dep.	....	....	6 8	....	6 47	7 3	7 15	....	7 30	7 42	7 57	....	8 22	....	8 34	....	8 39	....	....	....	9 2	....	9 9	....	9 37	9 57	1011	....	1027	1053	....	....
—	Dalston Junction...	....	....	6 15	....	6 54	7 10	7 25	....	7 40	7 49	8 3	....	8 29	....	8 40	....	8 46	....	....	....	9 9	....	9 14	....	9 44	10 4	1018	....	1034	11 0	....	....
—	Mildmay Park......	....	....	6 17	....	6 56	7 12	7 27	....	7 42	7 51	8 5	....	8 31	....	8 42	....	8 48	....	....	....	9 11	....	9 16	....	9 46	10 6	1020	....	1036	11 2	....	....
—	Canonbury	....	....	6 19	....	6 58	7 14	7 29	....	7 44	7 53	8 7	....	8 33	....	8 44	....	8 50	....	....	....	9 13	....	9 18	....	9 48	10 8	1022	....	1038	11 4	....	....
2½	Finsbury Park	5 35	5 40	6 24	6 47	7 12	7 21	7 34	7 42	7 49	7 59	8 13	8 27	8 38	8 40	8 49	8 52	8 55	9 3	9 5	9 9	9 18	9 22	9 27	9 38	9 55	1013	1030	1035	1043	11 9	1117	1135
3¼	Stroud Green	5 38	5 43	6 27	6 50	7 15	7 24	7 37	7 45	7 52	8 2	8 16	8 30	....	8 42	....	....	8 58	9 5	9 8	9 12	9 21	9 25	9 30	9 41	9 58	1016	1033	1038	1046	1112	1120	1138
3¾	Crouch End	5 41	5 46	6 30	6 53	7 18	7 27	7 40	7 48	7 55	8 5	8 19	8 33	8 43	8 45	....	....	9 1	....	9 11	9 15	9 24	9 28	9 33	9 44	10 1	1019	1036	1041	1049	1115	1123	1141
4¼	Highgate.............	5 45	5 50	6 34	6 56	7 22	7 31	7 44	7 52	7 59	8 9	8 23	8 37	....	8 52	8 55	....	9 4	....	9 15	9 18	9 28	9 32	9 37	9 48	10 5	1023	1040	1045	1053	1118	1126	1144
5¼	Cranley Gardens.....	....	....	....	....	....	....	....	....	8 2	....	8 26	....	....	....	....	....	....	....	....	9 21	9 31	....	....	9 51	....	1026	....	1048	1056	....	1129	....
6¼	Muswell Hill.........	5 49	....	....	....	....	....	....	....	8 4	....	8 28	....	....	....	....	9 2	....	9 15	....	9 23	9 33	....	....	9 53	....	1028	....	1050	1058	....	1131	....
6¾	Alexandra Palace.	....	....	....	....	....	....	....	....	....	....	....	....	....	....	....	....	....	....	....	9 25	....	....	....	9 56	....	1030	....	1052	11 0	....	1133	....
5¾	East Finchley........	....	5 54	6 38	6 59	7 26	7 35	7 48	7 56	....	8 13	....	8 41	8 49	8 56	....	....	....	....	9 19	....	....	....	9 41	....	10 9	....	1044	....	....	1122	....	1148
7¼	Finchley (Church End)	....	5 58	6 42	7 3	7 30	7 39	7 52	8 1	....	8 17	....	8 45	....	9 0	9 6	....	9 11	....	9 23	....	....	9 38	9 45	....	1013	....	1048	....	....	1126	....	1152
8¾	Mill Hill ‡ ¶¶........	....	....	....	....	....	7 42	....	8 8	....	8 38	....	....	....	9 4	....	....	....	....	9 33	....	....	....	....	....	1016	....	1051	....	....	1130	....	12 0
11¼	Edgware ....arr.	....	....	....	....	....	7 48	....	8 15	....	8 45	....	....	....	9 11	....	....	....	....	9 40	....	....	....	....	....	1023	....	1058	....	....	1137	....	12 7
8¾	Woodside Park §	....	6 2	6 46	7 7	7 34	7 42	....	8 5	....	8 21	....	8 49	....	....	....	....	9 15	....	9 27	....	....	9 41	9 49	....	1017	....	1052	....	....	1130	....	1156
9¾	Totteridge ‖	....	6 5	6 49	7 10	7 37	7 46	....	8 8	....	8 24	....	8 52	....	....	....	....	9 18	....	9 30	....	....	9 44	9 52	....	1020	....	1055	....	....	1133	....	1159
11¼	High Barnet .....arr.	....	6 10	6 54	7 14	7 41	7 51	....	8 12	....	8 29	....	8 56	....	....	9 13	....	9 22	....	9 34	....	....	9 48	9 57	....	1025	....	11 0	....	....	1137	....	12 3

Week Days—*Continued*.

Down.	mrn	mrn	aft	aft	aft	aft	aft	aft	aft	aft	aft	aft	aft	aft	aft	aft	aft	aft	aft	aft	aft	aft	aft	aft	aft	aft	aft	aft	aft	aft	aft	aft	aft
Moorgate Street.dep.	1121	1143	....	12 6	....	1216	1237	....	1247	1257	Sats. only.	1 9	1 13	Sats. only.	1 19	1 27	Sats. only.	1 36	1 45	Sats. only.	1 54	1 59	2 6	Sats. only.	2 15	Sats. only.	3 27	2e37	2 38	2 44	2 50	Sats. only.	....
Aldersgate Street....	1123	1145	....	12 8	....	1218	1239	....	1249	1259		1 11	1 15		1 21	1 29		1 38	1 47		1 56	2 1	2 8		2 17		2 29	2e39	2 40	2 46	2 52		....
Farringdon Street....	1125	1147	....	1210	....	1220	1241	....	1251	1 1		1 13	1 17		1 23	1 31		1 40	1 49		1 58	2 3	2 10		2 19		2 31	2e41	2 42	2 48	2 54		....
King's Cross (Met.)*..	1129	1151	....	1214	a	1224	1245	a	1255	1 5		1 17	1 21		1 27	1 35		1 44	1 53		2 2	2 7	2 14		2 23		2 35	2e45	2 46	2 52	2 58		....
" (Suburban) ...	1133	1155	12a1	1217	1222	1228	1248	1255	1258	1 9	1a15	1 20	....	1a27	1e32	....	1a44	1e47	....	2a2	2e5	2e10	....	2a24	....	2a32	2e38	2 48	2 50	2 55	3 2	3a8	3a18
Holloway †	1138	12 0	12 6	1222	....	1233	1252	....	1 2	1 13	....	1 24	....	....	1 35	1 41	....	1 51	1 59	2 7	2 9	2 14	2 20	....	2 32	2 37	2 43	2 53	....	3 0	3 6	3 13	3 22
Broad Street ¶ dep.	1127	....	1153	....	Sats. only.	1218	....	1242	Sats. only.	1 4	1 10	1 10	Sats. only.	1 18	1 25	Sats. only.	....	1s40	1 48	....	1s58	....	2 10	....	2 17	....	2 27	2 40	Sats. only.	2 47	2 55	....	....
Dalston Junction...	1134	....	12 0	....		1225	....	1249		1 9	1 15	1 17		1 25	1 30		....	1s45	1 55	....	2s3	....	2 15	....	2 24	....	2 34	2 45		2 54	3 0	....	....
Mildmay Park......	1136	....	12 2	....		1227	....	1251		1 11	....	1 19		1 27	1 32		....	....	1 57	....	....	....	....	....	2 26	....	2 36	2 47		2 56	3 2	....	....
Canonbury	1138	....	12 4	....		1230	....	1253		1 13	....	1 21		1 29	1 34		....	....	1 59	....	....	....	....	....	2 28	....	2 38	2 49		2 58	3 4	....	....
Finsbury Park.......	1144	12 6	12 9	1225	1228	1236	1255	1 1	1 14	1 18	1 22	1 28	1 30	1 34	1 39	1 44	1 50	1 54	2 4	2 10	2 13	2 17	2 25	2 32	2 35	2 40	2 46	2 56	2 59	3 4	3 11	3 18	3 25
Stroud Green.........	1147	12 9	1212	1228	1231	1239	1258	1 4	1 17	1 21	1 25	1 31	1 33	1 37	1 42	1 47	1 53	1 57	2 7	2 13	2 16	2 20	2 28	2 35	2 38	2 43	2 49	2 59	3 3	3 7	3 14	3 21	3 28
Crouch End...........	1150	1212	1215	1231	1234	1242	1 1	1 8	1 20	1 24	1 28	1 34	1 36	1 40	1 45	1 50	1 56	2 0	2 10	2 16	2 19	2 23	2 31	2 38	2 41	2 46	2 52	3 2	3 6	3 10	3 17	3 24	3 31
Highgate.............	1154	1215	1219	1235	1238	1246	1 4	1 12	1 24	1 28	1 32	1 38	1 40	1 44	1 49	1 54	2 0	2 4	2 14	2 20	2 22	2 27	2 35	2 42	2 45	2 50	2 56	3 6	3 10	3 14	3 20	3 28	3 34
Cranley Gardens...	1157	1218	....	....	1241	....	1 7	....	....	1 31	....	Except Sats.	1 43	....	1 52	....	....	2 7	Sats. only	2 23	....	2 30	Sats. only	2 45	Sats. only	3 53	....	3 9	....	3 17	....	3 31	....
Muswell Hill.......	1159	1220	....	....	1243	....	1 9	....	....	1 33	....		1 45	....	1 54	....	....	2 9		2 25	....	2 32		2 47		2 55	....	3 11	....	3 19	....	3 33	....
Alexandra Palace.	12 1	1222	....	....	1245	....	1 11	....	....	1 36	....		1 47	....	1 56	....	....	2 12		2 28	....	2 34		2 49		2 58	....	3 14	....	3 22	....	3 36	....
East Finchley........	....	....	1223	1239	....	1250	....	1 16	1 28	Saturdays only.	1 36	1 42	....	1 48	....	1 58	2 4	....	2 18	....	2 25	....	2 39	....	2 49	....	3 0	....	3 14	Saturdays only.	3 23	....	3 37
Finchley (Church End)	....	....	1228	1243	....	1253	....	1 20	....		1 40	1 46	....	1 52	....	2 2	2 8	....	2 22	....	2 29	....	2 43	....	2 53	....	3 4	....	3 19		3 27	....	3 41
Mill Hill ‡ ¶¶.......	....	....	....	....	....	1s1	....	1e26	....		....	....	....	1 57	....	....	....	....	2 27	....	2e32	....	....	....	2 56	....	....	....	....		3 30	....	....
Edgware ....arr.	....	....	....	....	....	1s8	....	1e33	....		....	....	....	2 4	....	....	....	....	2 34	....	2e39	....	....	....	3 3	....	....	....	....		3 37	....	....
Woodside Park §	....	....	1232	1247	....	1257	....	1 24	....		1 44	1 50	....	1 56	....	2 6	2 12	....	2 26	....	2 33	....	2 47	....	2 57	....	3 8	....	3 22		3 31	....	3 45
Totteridge ‖	....	....	1235	1250	....	1 0	....	1 27	....		1 47	1 53	....	1 59	....	2 9	2 15	....	2 29	....	2 36	....	2 50	....	3 0	....	3 11	....	3 25		3 34	....	3 48
High Barnet.......arr.	....	....	1240	1254	....	1 5	....	1 32	....		1 51	1 57	....	2 3	....	2 14	2 20	....	2 34	....	2 40	....	2 55	....	3 5	....	3 16	....	3 30		3 38	....	3 52

a Depart from Local Station Platform. b Depart from Main Line Platform. e Except Saturdays. s Saturdays only.

* Tickets are not issued at the Metropolitan Station at King's Cross to Passengers desirous of commencing their journey at that Station; such Passengers must travel by the Trains leaving the G. N. Co's. Local Sta. † Holloway & Caledonian Rd. ‡ About 2¼ miles to Midland Sta. § Station for North Finchley; ‖ for Whetstone.

¶ Nearly all Trains call at Shoreditch 2 minutes and Haggerston 5 minutes after leaving Broad Street.

¶¶ "Halt" at The Hale, between Mill Hill and Edgware.

June 1908

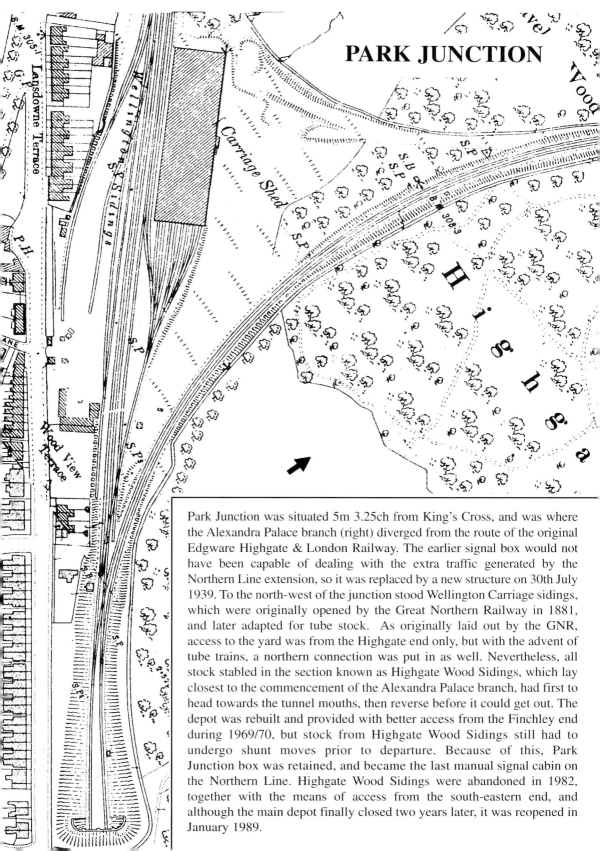

PARK JUNCTION

Park Junction was situated 5m 3.25ch from King's Cross, and was where the Alexandra Palace branch (right) diverged from the route of the original Edgware Highgate & London Railway. The earlier signal box would not have been capable of dealing with the extra traffic generated by the Northern Line extension, so it was replaced by a new structure on 30th July 1939. To the north-west of the junction stood Wellington Carriage sidings, which were originally opened by the Great Northern Railway in 1881, and later adapted for tube stock. As originally laid out by the GNR, access to the yard was from the Highgate end only, but with the advent of tube trains, a northern connection was put in as well. Nevertheless, all stock stabled in the section known as Highgate Wood Sidings, which lay closest to the commencement of the Alexandra Palace branch, had first to head towards the tunnel mouths, then reverse before it could get out. The depot was rebuilt and provided with better access from the Finchley end during 1969/70, but stock from Highgate Wood Sidings still had to undergo shunt moves prior to departure. Because of this, Park Junction box was retained, and became the last manual signal cabin on the Northern Line. Highgate Wood Sidings were abandoned in 1982, together with the means of access from the south-eastern end, and although the main depot finally closed two years later, it was reopened in January 1989.

59. Park Junction is viewed from a train on 3rd July 1954, the last day of service on the Alexandra Palace line. The 1939 signal box can just be seen to the right, whilst in the middle distance, between the diverging routes stands the carriage sheds of Wellington Sidings. (Alan A. Jackson)

60. We now see Park Junction signal box, derelict and surrounded by the encroaching trees of Highgate Wood. When opened it had seventy-four working levers and nine spare. After falling into disuse it became the haunt of drug addicts and the suchlike, and was finally demolished in 1995. (J.E. Connor)

61.   The course of the Alexandra Palace branch trackbed through Highgate Wood became heavily overgrown, but there were still a few remains of railway interest, such as these concrete posts for LT lineside cabling near Park Junction in 1994. (J.E. Connor)

62.   We remain in 1994, and see a bridge which carried a footpath over the trackbed south of Cranley Gardens. (J.E. Connor)

CRANLEY GARDENS

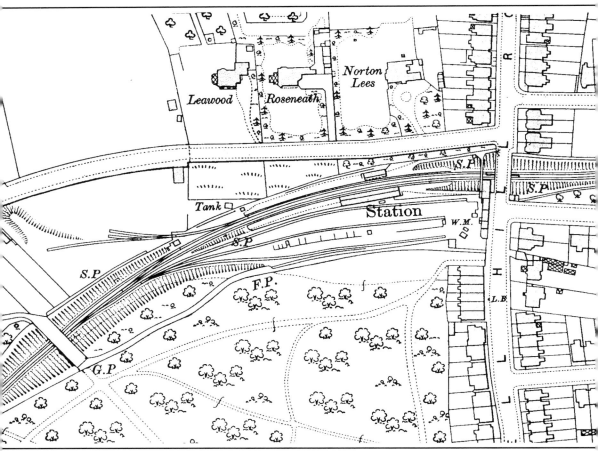

Suburban growth in the area around Muswell Hill resulted in a new passenger station being opened at Cranley Gardens on 2nd August 1902. It adjoined a goods yard, which had been brought into use five years earlier.

During the construction of Fortis Hill Reservoir in 1906/7, some track was laid behind the signal box on the down side, and was used by contractors, who provided their own locomotives. Although some of this was lifted when the job was completed, the remainder was retained as Metropolitan Water Board private sidings, and was still listed as such in 1938.

The fortunes of Cranley Gardens station were badly affected by the competition offered by road transport, and traffic was in decline less than two decades after opening. Surveys held by the GNR revealed that whilst 12,948 ordinary tickets were purchased there in March 1914, only 5,995 were sold during the same month five years later.

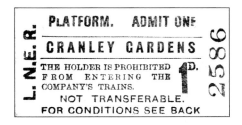

L.N.E.R. PLATFORM. ADMIT ONE

CRANLEY GARDENS

THE HOLDER IS PROHIBITED FROM ENTERING THE COMPANY'S TRAINS. 1D.

NOT TRANSFERABLE. FOR CONDITIONS SEE BACK

2586

3. A view from the bridge shown in the previous photograph, shows the Metropolitan Water Board's ortis Hill pumping station to the left of Cranley Gardens signal box, and tracks leading to the goods yard n the right. (Lens of Sutton)

4. View from a down train entering the station on the last day of public service. The goods yard appears o be busy with coal traffic, whilst the ex-GNR somersault signal is in the 'off' position, and indicates that he signal box had been switched out. (Alan A. Jackson)

65.   We look northwards along Muswell Hill Road in the first decade of the twentieth century to see th goods yard entrance on the left, with the coal offices and passenger station adjoining. (Lens of Sutton)

KING'S CROSS, FINSBURY PARK, ALEXANDRA PALACE, HIGH BARNET 🆅 THIRD CLASS ONLY 🆅

WEEKDAYS

				SX	SO		SX	SO				SO				SO	SX	SX	SO	SX	SO		SO	SO	SO
		a.m.	a.m.	a.m.	a.m.	a.m.	a.m.	a.m.		a.m.		a.m.	a.m.	a.m.	a.m.	a.m.	a.m.	a.m.	a.m.	a.m.	a.m.	a.m.	a.m.	p.m.	p.m.
A { KING'S CROSS .. .. .. dep.	6 5	..	6 53	6 55	..	7 24	7 24	7T50	..	8 10	..	8 28	..	8 50	..	..	9 45	10 3	10 3	1045	1050	11 8	1118	..	1145	12 9	1230
{ Finsbury Park — — — — arr.	6 11	..	6 59	7 2	..	7 30	7 30	7T56	..	8 16	..	8 34	..	8 56	..	..	9 51	10 9	10 9	1051	1056	1114	1125	..	1151	1215	1236
FINSBURY PARK .. .. .. dep.	6 20	—	7 0	7 20	—	7 40	7 40	8 0	8 18	8 18	—	8 35	—	9 0	9 17	9 40	—	10 0	1020	1030	11 0	1120	1130	1140	—	12 0	1222	1240
Stroud Green — — — — ,,	6 23	—	7 3	7 23	—	7 43	7 43	8 3	8 21	8 21	—	8 38	—	9 3	9 20	9 43	—	10 3	1023	1033	11 3	1123	1133	1143	—	12 3	1225	1243
Crouch End .. — — — ,,	6 26	—	7 6	7 26	—	7 46	7 46	8 6	8 24	8 24	—	8 41	—	9 6	9 23	9 46	—	10 6	1026	1036	11 6	1126	1136	1146	—	12 6	1228	1246
Highgate — — — — ,,	6 30	—	7 10	7 30	—	7 50	7 50	8 10	8 28	8 28	—	8 45	—	9 10	9 27	9 50	—	1010	1030	1040	1110	1130	1140	1150	—	1210	1232	1250
Cranley Gardens.. — — — ,,	..	—	7 13	7 33	—	7 53	7 53	8 13	8 31	8 31	—	8 48	—	9 13	9 30	9 53	/..	1013	1033	1043	1113	1133	1143	1153	—	1213	1235	1253
Muswell Hill — — — ,,	..	—	7 15	7 35	—	7 55	7 55	8 15	8 33	8 33	—	8 50	—	9 15	9 32	9 55	—	1015	1035	1045	1115	1135	1145	1155	—	1215	1237	1255
ALEXANDRA PALACE.. .. arr.	..	—	7 17	7 37	—	7 57	7 57	8 17	8 35	8 35	—	8 52	—	9 17	9 34	9 57	—	1017	1037	1047	1117	1137	1147	1157	—	1217	1239	1257
B { Highgate — — — — dep.	6 41	—	7 18	7 33	—	7 53	7 55	8 13	8 33	8 37	—	8 49	—	9 13	9 33	9 55	—	1013	1033	1043	1113	1133	1143	1155	—	1213	1236	1256
{ East Finchley .. .. arr.	6 44	—	7 21	7 36	—	7 56	7 58	8 16	8 36	8 40	—	8 52	—	9 16	9 36	9 58	—	1016	1036	1046	1116	1136	1146	1158	—	1216	1239	1259
{ Finchley Central— — — ,,	6 47	—	7 24	7 40	—	7 59	8 1	8 19	8 40	8 43	—	8 55	—	9 19	9 39	10 1	—	1019	1041	1049	1119	1139	1149	12 1	—	1219	1242	1
{ Mill Hill East — — ,,	6E57	—	7 34	7 43	—	8 3	8 6	8 23	8 43	8 49	—	9 3	—	9 28	9 42	1016	—	1028	1044	1059	1129	1142	1159	1210	—	1222	1245	6
{ West Finchley — — — ,,	6 49	—	7 26	7 45	—	8 4	8 9	8 24	8 43	8 45	—	8 57	—	9 21	9 47	10 3	—	1021	1049	1051	1121	1149	1151	12 3	—	1227	1248	7
{ Woodside Park for N. Finchley ,,	6 51	—	7 29	7 47	—	8 6	8 11	8 45	8 45	8 47	—	8 59	—	9 23	9 49	10 5	—	1023	1051	1053	1123	1151	1153	12 5	—	1229	1250	9
{ Totteridge & Whetstone — ,,	6 54	—	7 32	7 50	—	8 9	8 14	8 29	8 48	8 50	—	9 2	—	9 26	9 52	10 8	—	1026	1054	1056	1126	1154	1156	12 8	—	1232	1253	12
{ HIGH BARNET .. .. ,,	6 58	—	7 35	7 53	—	8 12	8 17	8 32	8 52	8 53	—	9 5	—	9 30	9 55	1011	—	1030	1057	1059	1129	1157	1159	1211	—	1236	1257	16

WEEKDAYS—continued

		SO	SO		SO	SO		SO	SO		SX	SO			SX	SX	SX	SX	SX		SX	SX	
		p.m.	p.m.		p.m.	p.m.		p.m.	p.m.	p.m.	p.m.	p.m.	p.m.			p.m.	p.m.	p.m.	p.m.	p.m.		p.m.	p.m.	
A { KING'S CROSS .. .. dep.	1 15	—	..	1 50	2 0	..	2 15	2 45	3 10	3 50	..	4 10	4 22	..	4 30	4 50	..	4 50	5 13	5 34	5 52	6 13	..	6 25	6 45	A	..
{ Finsbury Park — — — arr.	1 21	—	..	1 56	2 6	..	2 21	2 51	3 17	3 56	..	4 17	4 28	..	4 36	4 56	..	4 56	5 19	5 40	5 58	6 19	..	6 31	6 51		..
FINSBURY PARK .. .. dep.	1 22	1 40	—	2 0	2 20	—	2 40	3 0	3 20	4 0	—	4 20	4 30	—	4 40	5 0	—	5 0	5 23	5 43	6 0	6 23	—	6 40	7 0		NO
Stroud Green — — — ,,	1 25	1 43	—	2 3	2 23	—	2 43	3 3	3 23	4 3	—	4 23	4 33	—	4 43	5 3	—	5 3	5 26	5 46	6 3	6 26	—	6 43	7 3		SUNDAY
Crouch End .. — — — ,,	1 28	1 46	—	2 6	2 26	—	2 46	3 6	3 26	4 6	—	4 26	4 36	—	4 46	5 6	—	5 6	5 29	5 49	6 6	6 29	—	6 46	7 6		SERVICE
Highgate — — — — ,,	1 32	1 50	—	2 10	2 30	—	2 50	3 10	3 30	4 10	—	4 30	4 40	—	4 50	5 10	—	5 10	5 33	5 53	6 10	6 33	—	6 50	7 10		
Cranley Gardens.. — — — ,,	1 35	1 53	—	2 13	2 33	—	2 53	3 13	3 33	4 13	—	4 33	4 43	—	4 53	5 13	—	5 13	5 36	5 56	6 13	6 36	—	6 53	7 13		
Muswell Hill — — — ,,	1 37	1 55	—	2 15	2 35	—	2 55	3 15	3 35	4 15	—	4 35	4 45	—	4 55	5 15	—	5 15	5 38	5 58	6 15	6 38	—	6 55	7 15		
ALEXANDRA PALACE.. arr.	1 39	1 57	—	2 17	2 37	—	2 57	3 17	3 37	4 17	—	4 37	4 47	—	4 57	5 17	—	5 17	5 40	6 0	6 17	6 40	—	6 57	7 17		
B { Highgate — — — dep.	1 37	1 55	—	2 13	2 35	—	2 58	3 13	3 36	4 13	—	4 33	4 43	—	4 53	5 13	—	5 14	5 36	5 57	6 14	6 36	—	6 54	7 14		—
{ East Finchley .. .. arr.	1 40	1 58	—	2 16	2 38	—	3 1	3 16	3 40	4 16	—	4 36	4 46	—	4 56	5 16	—	5 17	5 39	6 0	6 17	6 39	—	6 57	7 17		..
{ Finchley Central— — — ,,	1 43	2 1	—	2 19	2 41	—	3 4	3 19	3 43	4 19	—	4 39	4 49	—	5 0	5 19	—	5 20	5 42	6 4	6 20	6 42	—	7 0	7 21	B	..
{ Mill Hill East — — ,,	1 46	2 11	—	2 29	2 44	—	3 14	3 29	3 44	4 29	—	4 42	4 59	—	5 3	5 29	—	5 23	5 52	6 14	6 29	6 52	—	7 4	7 28		..
{ West Finchley — — — ,,	1 49	2 3	—	2 21	2 51	—	3 6	3 21	3 51	4 21	—	4 47	4 51	—	5 24	5 44	—	6 6	6 26	6 45	—	7 6	7 22		..		
{ Woodside Park for N. Finchley ,,	1 51	2 5	—	2 23	2 53	—	3 8	3 23	3 53	4 23	—	4 50	4 53	—	5 6	5 26	—	6 26	6 45	—	7 8	7 24		..		
{ Totteridge & Whetstone — ,,	1 54	2 8	—	2 26	2 56	—	3 11	3 26	3 56	4 26	—	4 52	4 56	—	5 9	5 26	—	6 26	6 50	—	7 11	7 29		..		
{ HIGH BARNET .. .. ,,	1 57	2 11	—	2 30	2 59	—	3 14	3 29	3 59	4 29	—	4 54	4 59	—	5 12	5 29	—	5 33	5 36	6 14	6 33	6 53	—	7 14	7 31		..

A Passengers from King's Cross change at Finsbury Park.

B Electric Service: change at Highgate. A frequent service of Underground (Northern Line) trains is available on Weekdays and Sundays between King's Cros (L.T.E.) and these stations.

E Change also at Finchley Central.	S or SO Saturdays only.	SX Saturdays excepted.	T On Saturdays runs 5 minutes earlier

5.   Here we see the street level building around 1935. Herbert Clarke whose coal office stands to the left, so had premises adjoining the station at Crouch End. (LT Museum)

67.   We take a look at the station towards Alexandra Palace in GNR days. In addition to the main entrance, there was also a supplementary exit, which led from the down platform to the corner of Woodside Avenue. (Lens of Sutton)

68.   This is the up side during the same period, showing the slope which was employed as access to and from the street level building. The crossover was used in connection with goods traffic entering or leaving the adjacent yard. (Lens of Sutton)

69.   We again look along the platforms towards Alexandra Palace, but this time during the 1930s. The station remained gas-lit until its closure. (Lens of Sutton)

70.   Class C12 4-4-2T No.7374 stands at the station with the Finsbury Park - Alexandra Palace shuttle in the late 1940s. Evidence of the unfinished electrification can be seen on the up line. (Photographer Unknown/Author's Collection)

71.   As we look towards Highgate in the early 1950s, we see that the station was still well kept, although the crossover had been removed. (Stations UK)

72.   This is the country end of the up platform seen from a train on 3rd July 1954. The surrounding foliage gave the station an almost rural appearance. (Alan A. Jackson)

73.   On the last day at Cranley Gardens, we see an N2-hauled Finsbury Park-Alexandra Palace train standing at the down platform. (Alan A. Jackson)

74.   As we look towards Alexandra Palace on 23rd March 1957, we notice that although the station was beginning to get overgrown, the track still remained free of weeds. Platform modifications carried out in connection with the proposed extension of the Northern Line are evident on the up side. (Alan A. Jackson)

75.   After closure to passengers, the line was retained for freight traffic, with goods trains running as far as Cranley Gardens until 1957. A year later the track was lifted, and a general air of dereliction began to set in. The passenger station remained near enough intact for a while, but vandals eventually set about wrecking it. This is a post-closure view from the west side of Muswell Hill Road, with the former station footbridge in the foreground. The closest pair of concrete posts on the up platform once held the running-in nameboard, whilst the other supported a 'Way Out' sign. (B.P. Pask)

76. Here we see the street level building soon after closure. It was located on the west side of Muswell Hill Road, almost opposite the junction with Cranley Gardens. (B.P. Pask)

77. This is the same building in 1967, not long before it was demolished. Although it remained firmly locked, it was still possible to peep through a broken window, and see a pre-1954 Underground map on one of the interior walls. By this time all the roofing slates had gone, and the adjoining coal offices had been damaged by fire. (I. Baker)

78. By 1965, the entire station area was overgrown, and had become a dumping place for unwanted items, such as the rusting car seen to the left. Everything had been vandalised, although the former up side building still retained a recognisable form. (J.E. Connor)

79. From beneath the up side awning, we see that that although the building's front wall was still standing, little remained behind. Demolition finally came at the end of the 1960s, and the site was subsequently redeveloped as a school. (J.E. Connor)

NORTH-EAST OF CRANLEY GARDENS

0.   The seventeen-arch brick viaduct between Cranley Gardens and Muswell Hill, which till survives, carried the formation above St. James' Lane. This view was taken in 1972. (. Baker/Connor & Butler Collection)

1.   The trackbed over the viaduct, which is now used as a footpath, provides an excellent view of the London skyline. (J.E. Connor)

KING'S CROSS, FINSBURY PARK, ALEXANDRA PALACE

THIRD CLASS ONLY

WEEKDAYS ONLY

		a.m.		a.m.		a.m.		a.m.		a.m.	SX	SO	a.m.		a.m.		a.m.		SO		SO		SO		S
											a.m.	a.m.							a.m.		p.m.		p.m.		p.
A { KING'S CROSS .. .. dep.		6 5	..	6 53	..	6 55	..	7 24	..	7 40	7 54	8 8	8 29	..	8 54	..	8 59	..	11 54	..	12 9	..	12 29	..	12
Finsbury Park — .. —arr.		6 11	..	6 59	..	7 2	..	7 30	..	7 46	8 0	8 14	8 35	..	9 0	..	9 5	..	12 0	..	12 15	..	12 35	..	12
FINSBURY PARK .. .. ..dep.		6 20	..	7 0	..	7 20	..	7 40	..	8 0	8 18	8 18	8 38	..	9 2	..	9 17	..	12 2	..	12 22	..	12 40	..	I
Stroud Green .. .. .. ,,		6 23	..	7 3	..	7 23	..	7 43	..	8 3	8 21	8 21	8 41	..	9 5	..	9 20	..	12 5	..	12 25	..	12 43	..	I
Crouch End .. .. .. ,,		6 26	..	7 6	..	7 26	..	7 46	..	8 6	8 24	8 24	8 44	..	9 8	..	9 23	..	12 8	..	12 28	..	12 46	..	I
Highgate .. .. .. ,,		6 30	..	7 10	..	7 30	..	7 50	..	8 10	8 28	8 28	8 48	..	9 12	..	9 27	..	12 12	..	12 32	..	12 50	..	I
Cranley Gardens.. .. .. ,,		—	..	7 13	..	7 33	..	7 53	..	8 13	8 31	8 31	8 51	..	9 15	..	9 30	..	12 15	..	12 35	..	12 53	..	I
Muswell Hill .. .. .. ,,		—	..	7 15	..	7 35	..	7 55	..	8 15	8 33	8 33	8 53	..	9 17	..	9 32	..	12 17	..	12 37	..	12 55	..	I
ALEXANDRA PALACE.. .. arr.		..	..	7 17	..	7 37	..	7 57	..	8 17	8 35	8 35	8 55	..	9 19	..	9 34	..	12 19	..	12 39	..	12 57	..	I

WEEKDAYS ONYL—continued

		SO	SO		SO	SO		SO		SO		SX SO		SX			SX	SX		SX		SX		SX
		p.m.	p.m.		p.m.	p.m.		p.m.		p.m.		p.m. p.m.		p.m.			p.m.	p.m.		p.m.		p.m.		p.m.
A { KING'S CROSS .. .. dep.		1 15	1 29		1 54	..		2 21		2 54		3 54 4 10		4 29	4 54	..	5 13	5 33	..	5 54	..	6 14	..	6 25
Finsbury Park — .. —arr.		1 21	1 35		2 0	..		2 27		3 0		4 0 4 17	4 17	4 35	5 0	..	5 19	5 39	..	6 0	..	6 20	..	6 31
FINSBURY PARK .. .. ..dep.		1 22	1 40		2 2	2 20		2 40		3 2		4 2 4 22	4 32	4 40	5 2	..	5 22	5 40	..	6 3	..	6 22	..	6 40
Stroud Green .. .. .. ,,		1 25	1 43		2 5	2 23		2 43		3 5		4 5 4 25	4 35	4 43	5 5	..	5 25	5 43	..	6 6	..	6 25	..	6 43
Crouch End .. .. .. ,,		1 28	1 46		2 8	2 26		2 46		3 8		4 8 4 28	4 38	4 46	5 8	..	5 28	5 46	..	6 9	..	6 28	..	6 46
Highgate .. .. .. ,,		1 32	1 50		2 12	2 30		2 50		3 12		4 12 4 32	4 42	4 50	5 12	..	5 32	5 50	..	6 13	..	6 32	..	6 50
Cranley Gardens.. .. .. ,,		1 35	1 53		2 15	2 33		2 53		3 15		4 15 4 35	4 45	4 53	5 15	..	5 35	5 53	..	6 16	..	6 35	..	6 53
Muswell Hill .. .. .. ,,		1 37	1 55		2 17	2 35		2 55		3 17		4 17 4 37	4 47	4 55	5 17	..	5 37	5 55	..	6 18	..	6 37	..	6 55
ALEXANDRA PALACE.. .. arr.		1 39	1 57		2 19	2 37		2 57		3 19		4 19 4 39	4 49	4 57	5 19	..	5 39	5 57	..	6 20	..	6 39	..	6 57

A   Passengers from King's Cross change at Finsbury Park.

SO Saturdays only.   **SX** Saturdays excepted.

ALEXANDRA PALACE, FINSBURY PARK, KING'S CROSS

THIRD CLASS ONLY

WEEKDAYS ONLY

		a.m.		a.m.		a.m.		a.m.	SX	SO		SX	SO		SX	SO		SX	SO		a.m.		a.m.		FSX	FSO
									a.m.	a.m.		a.m.	a.m.		a.m.	a.m.		a.m.	a.m.						a.m.	a.m.
ALEXANDRA PALACE .. ..dep.		..	..	7 5	..	7 25	..	7 45	7 45	8 8		8 21	8 21		8 38	8 38		9 0	..	9 25	..	9 42	9 42			
Muswell Hill — — .. ,,		..	..	7 7	..	7 27	..	7 47	7 47	8 10		8 23	8 23		8 40	8 40		9 2	..	9 27	..	9 44	9 44			
Cranley Gardens.. — .. ,,		..	..	7 10	..	7 30	..	7 50	7 50	8 13		8 26	8 26		8 43	8 43		9 5	..	9 30	..	9 47	9 47			
Highgate — — — .. ,,		5 32	..	6 38	7 13	..	7 33	..	7 51	8 16		8 29	8 29		8 46	8 46		9 8	..	9 33	—	9 50	9 50			
Crouch End .. — — .. ,,		5 35	..	6 41	7 16	..	7 36	..	7 54	8 19		8 32	8 32		8 49	8 49		9 11	..	9 36	—	9 53	9 53			
Stroud Green — — .. ,,		5 37	..	6 43	7 18	..	7 38	..	7 56	8 21		8 34	8 34		8 51	8 51		9 13	..	9 38	—	9 55	9 55			
FINSBURY PARK .. .. arr.		5 39	..	6 45	7 20	..	7 40	..	7 58	8 23		8 36	8 36		8 53	8 53		9 15	..	9 40	—	9 57	9 57			
A { Finsbury Park — — —dep.		5 41	..	6 49	7J21	..	7 46	..	7 59	8 26		8 27		8 37	8 48		8 54	8 57		9 17	..	—	10 13	10 21			
KING'S CROSS .. .. arr.		5 47	..	6 58	7J27	..	7Y52	..	8 5	8 12		8 32	8Y34		8 43	8 54		9Y 0	9Y 3		9 23	..	—	10 20	10Y28			

WEEKDAYS ONLY—continued

		SO	SO		SO	SO		SO	SO		SO	SO		SO	SO	SX		SX	SO	SX		SX	FSX	FO	SX		SX	SX
		p.m.	p.m.		p.m.	p.m.		p.m.	p.m.		p.m.	p.m.		p.m.	p.m.	p.m.		p.m.	p.m.	p.m.		p.m.	p.m.	p.m.	p.m.		p.m.	p.m.
ALEXANDRA PALACE .. ..dep.		12 25	12 45	—	1 5	1 25		2 5	2 25		3 5	3 25		5 5	5 25	5 45		6 5	6 25	6 45	..	7 5	7 25			
Muswell Hill — — .. ,,		12 27	12 47	—	1 7	1 27		2 7	2 27		3 7	3 27	4 27	4 47	5 7	5 27	5 47		6 7	6 27	6 47	..	7 7	7 27			
Cranley Gardens.. — .. ,,		12 30	12 50	—	1 10	1 30		2 10	2 30		3 10	3 30	4 30	4 50	5 10	5 30	5 50		6 10	6 30	6 50	..	7 10	7 30			
Highgate — — — .. ,,		12 33	12 53	—	1 31	1 33	1 53		2 13	2 33	2 53		3 13	3 33	4 33	4 53	5 13	5 33	5 53		6 13	6 33	6 53	..	7 13	7 33		
Crouch End .. — — .. ,,		12 36	12 56	—	1 16	1 36	1 56		2 16	2 36	2 56		3 16	3 36	4 36	4 56	5 16	5 36	5 56		6 16	6 36	6 56	..	7 16	7 36		
Stroud Green — — .. ,,		12 38	12 58	—	1 18	1 38	1 58		2 18	2 38	2 58		3 18	3 38	4 38	4 58	5 18	5 38	5 58		6 18	6 38	6 58	..	7 18	7 38		
FINSBURY PARK .. .. arr.		12 40	1 0	—	1 20	1 40	2 0		2 20	2 40	3 0		3 20	3 40	4 40	5 0	5 20	5 40	6 0		6 20	6 40	6 40	7 0	..	7 20	7 40	
A { Finsbury Park — — —dep.		12 52	1 16	—		1 44	2 14			3 21	3 52	4 56	5 14	5X21	5 47	5 26	6 12		..	6 21	6 44	6 50	7A 7	—	7 21	7 56	
KING'S CROSS .. .. arr.		1Y 0	1Y22	..		1Y50	2Y20			3Y28	3Y58	5 4	4Y20	5X27	5Y54	5 58	6 22		..	6Z31	6 50	6 56	7A13	—	7Z28	8 8	

A   Passengers to King's Cross change at Finsbury Park.

A On Fridays runs 5 minutes later.   **FSX** Fridays and Saturdays excepted.   **SO** Saturdays only.   **Y** King's Cross (York Road) station.
FO Fridays only.   **J** On Saturdays runs 3 minutes later.   **SX** Saturdays excepted.   **Z** King's Cross (York Road) on Fridays.
FSO Fridays and Saturdays only.

Summer 1951

MUSWELL HILL

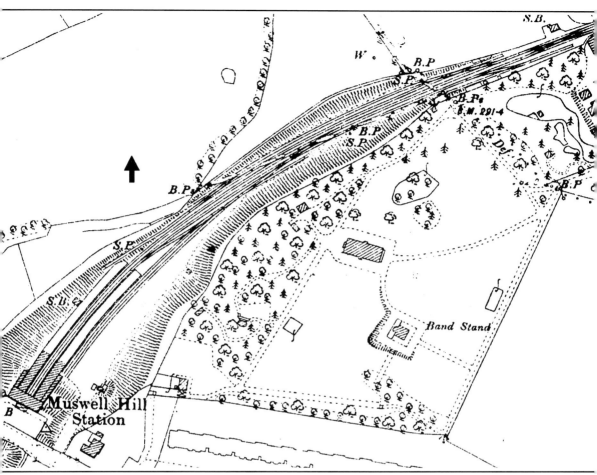

Situated 6miles 14.5chains from King's Cross, the station was opened along with the branch from Park Junction in 1873. There was a two-road coal yard behind the up plat-form, but as the points faced Alexandra Palace, trains from the London direction had to go through the station, and reverse before gaining access. Apart from high days and holidays at the Palace, Muswell Hill was always the busiest station on the branch, as it was well positioned to attract commuters from the surrounding suburb. However, when surveyed in 1894, much of the district still remained largely undeveloped. The close proximity between Muswell Hill and the terminus is emphasised on the map by the fact that the Alexandra Palace signal box appears near the top right.

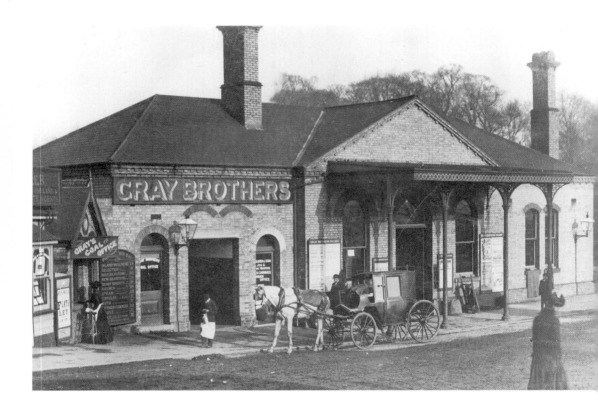

82.   The street level building was sited on the north side of Muswell Hill, and set back slightly behind a small forecourt. Access to the two platforms was by means of covered stairways from the booking hall. During the various periods when Alexandra Palace station was closed, Muswell Hill was used as the branch terminus. When first opened, it formed the boundary of the GNR, as until 1911, the tracks beyond belonged to the nominally independent Muswell Hill & Palace Railway. To improve passenger flow at Muswell Hill, a passimeter booking office was opened within the street level building in 1927, but otherwise the station remained virtually unaltered throughout its life. This view dates from the turn of the century. (Lens of Sutton)

83.   Here we look towards Alexandra Palace in the early years of the present century. In addition
to passenger access by way of the street level building, there was also a peak hour exit to Duke's
Avenue which led from the down side, near the footbridge seen in the middle distance. (Lens of Sutton)

84.   A class N2 0-6-2T enters the station with a train from either Moorgate or Kings Cross to Alexandra
Palace in LNER days.(Stations UK)

85. Ex-GCR class F2 2-4-2T No.5785 steams away from Muswell Hill with the push-pull service from Finsbury Park. Conductor rails are in position on part of the main formation, whilst the tracks leading to the coal yard can be seen in the foreground. The view must pre-date August 1946, as the locomotive was renumbered 7113 at that time. (Real Photographs Co. Ltd.)

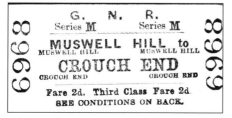

86.   A view from the footbridge towards Highgate before nationalisation gives us a good overall impression of the station. One of the covered stairways providing access from the street level building can be clearly seen. (Stations UK)

87.   A later view in the same direction, with the signal box on the down platform now minus its nameboard. The shell of an unfinished electrical sub-station, erected in connection with the 1935 New Works Scheme stands to the left of the picture, behind the wagons in the coal yard. (Stations UK)

88.   Class N2/4 No.69571 waits at Muswell Hill with a train for Alexandra Palace, possibly on the las[t] day of passenger services. Many of the N2s, including this one, were equipped with condensing apparatu[s] so that they could work over the Metropolitan Widened Lines to Moorgate. (Author's Collection)

89.   On the last day, we look down from the footbridge, and see an up train departing for Finsbury Park[.] (Alan A. Jackson)

90. This is the street level building at Muswell Hill after closure. Comparison with view No.82 reveals he various minor alterations which took place since pre-grouping times. (B.P. Pask)

91. All workings over the Park Junction - Alexandra Palace branch ceased in 1957, and the track was lifted the following year. The buildings at Muswell Hill station disappeared soon afterwards, possibly in 1960, when the road bridge over the formation was strengthened to take double-deck buses. The platforms were finally removed about 1966. (Photomatic)

ALEXANDRA PALACE

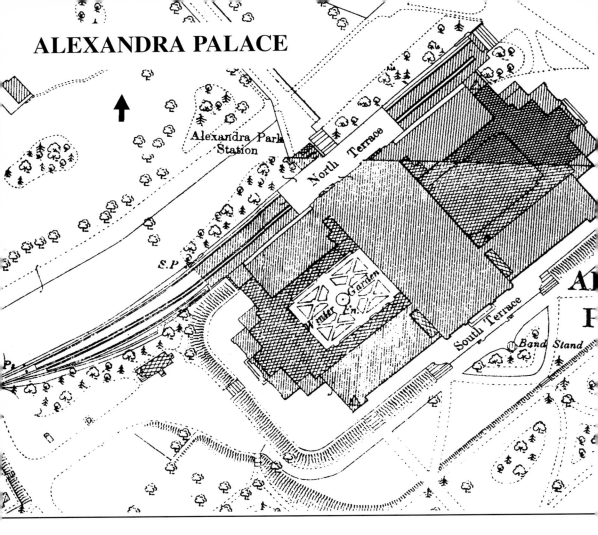

The station entrance was located at the south-eastern end of a road known as The Avenue, and was totally dwarfed by the huge bulk of the Palace building which it adjoined.

When first opened it comprised two wooden platforms, which were protected for some of their length by a terrace situated beside the north-western facade of the Palace itself. By the early years of the twentieth century these were suffering from decay, and the decision was made that the station should be rebuilt. A new island platform with umbrella awning was constructed, and the majority of terrace removed, leaving just a flight of steps adjoining the station entrance.

Coal to heat the Palace invariably arrived by rail, and a two-road siding was provided chiefly for this purpose. However, apart from this the station had no goods facilities.

The Ordnance Survey Plan above shows the area as it was in 1894, during one of the periods that branch passenger services had been cut-back to Muswell Hill. The station was renamed Alexandra Park in 1891, when the GNR were hoping to attract more residential traffic, but it closed again the following year. It was reopened on a more permanent basis in 1898, and reverted to its original name.

The reason for the station's lack of patronage was that the surrounding area was comparatively slow to develop, as indicated on the map. Even as late as March 1914 there was only 4,392 ordinary bookings from Alexandra Palace, and these fell to 2,622 when a similar survey was held five years later.

THE PALACE

Following the success of the Crystal Palace at Sydenham, a group of businessmen proposed that a similar venture could be undertaken in north London. They chose a 240 acre site at Muswell Hill, and announced that the new development was to be known as the Alexandra Palace.

The first section of the grounds was brought into public use in connection with a Flower Show on 23rd July 1863, when the surrounding parkland was officially opened by Alexandra, Princess of Wales. However, the construction of the 'Palace' itself did not start until the following year.

The huge building was designed by architect J. Johnson, in collaboration with engineer M. Meeson, and was constructed by the firm of Messrs. Kelk and Lucas. It was an immense task, and required a force of around 1,000 men to work on site.

In 1868, a racecourse was opened in the grounds, but, although structurally well advanced at this time, the main complex had to wait another five years before it was deemed ready for the public.

The official opening of Alexandra Palace was performed by the Lord Mayor of London on 24th May 1873, and within a fortnight it had been visited by 124,124 people. Many of these would have travelled by train, as the branch from Highgate was brought into use on the same day as the Palace itself.

Just weeks after, disaster struck in the early afternoon of Monday 9th June, when the building was totally gutted by fire, and subsequently closed. Rebuilding was soon in hand, and within two years a completely new edifice arose from the ashes.

Sadly the development's fortunes were soon in decline, and the owning company found itself in severe financial difficulties. As the section of branch line beyond Muswell Hill only served the Palace, and conveyed very little residential traffic, it was closed on a number of occasions, although with the growth of suburbia prospects for it began to improve.

In addition to the Alexandra Palace branch, the area was also served by stations at Wood Green (GNR), and Palace Gates (GER), although the latter was rather misleadingly named, as it

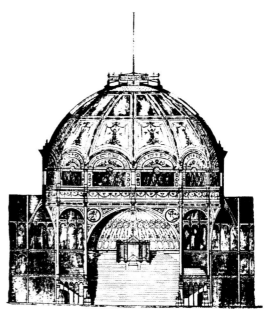

The Engineer 15.3.1867

presented the unfamiliar visitor with a long up-hill walk before reaching the Palace! A remedy of sorts appeared in 1898 however, when an electric tramway was opened, which linked the Park gates near Wood Green station with the main complex, 660yds away. This closed after just eighteen months, but with the early twentieth century enthusiasm for trams it was not long before more permanent routes were introduced to the district.

Throughout its long history, Alexandra Palace had a very chequered career, and has been admired by some, whilst disliked by others. With the exception of the war years, part of it housed the Television Centre of the BBC from the late 1930s until 1956, and the rooftop mast once provided a familiar logo which was seen at the start of TV news broadcasts. The Greater London Council resolved to demolish the Great Hall in the 1960s, but the decision was revoked in 1970.

Another serious fire occurred in July 1980, and although badly damaged, the building was again repaired, and it remains to this day, possibly qualifying as north London's most distinctive landmark.

92.   This is the original layout of Alexandra Palace station, as it appeared in June 1873, after the Palace had been gutted by fire. A report on the incident in The Illustrated London News read : *"The cause of the fire was the carelessness of workmen employed to repair the leadwork in the roof of the great dome. A morsel of red hot charcoal, dropped from a brazier, set fire to the timber and papier mache in a crevice where it fell near the upper gallery outside the dome, while the men were gone to dinner at half past twelve. In a few minutes, almost before the alarm could be given, the central part of the dome, inside as well as outside, was involved in flames which quickly spread in every direction till the whole vast building was consumed. The first outbreak within the building was observed by many persons, and shouts of alarm ran through the nave and transepts, while a multitude of visitors escaped as fast as they could by every door. Hydrants abounded in the main passages and galleries, many of these were operated by the attendants, but from the first it was discovered that no force of water was on, and all hope of arresting the progress of the fire was precluded. When the alarm reached the offices of the manager and secretary, the united efforts of their staff were devoted to rescuing from destruction the most valuable objects of art in the palace. The loan collection of modern pictures and drawings were torn from the gallery walls and carried by files of men out into the park."* (Greater London Council)

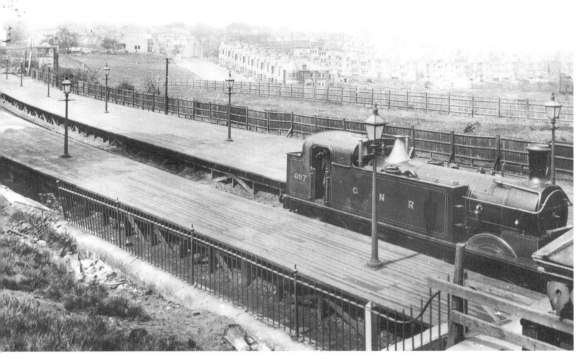

93.   GNR Stirling 0-4-4T No.697 awaits departure from Alexandra Palace, whilst the station was in its original form before rebuilding with a single island platform. (Pamlin Prints)

ALEXANDRA PALACE.—EASTER HOLIDAYS.
    Dr. HARLEY, the wonderful Deceptionist, in his marvellous Facial Metamorphosis Séance, PHYSIOGNOMANIA.

ALEXANDRA PALACE.—EASTER HOLIDAYS.
    MUSICAL and MIMICAL MONOLOGUE Interspersed with Recitals by Messrs. A. G. Pritchard and Harry Fancy.

ALEXANDRA PALACE.—EASTER HOLIDAYS.
    Palace and Grounds Brilliantly Illuminated by the largest combined Electric Light Installation in Europe. Gulcher Company. 1s.

ALEXANDRA PALACE.—EASTER HOLIDAYS.
    REFRESHMENTS, under the personal control of the Administration, prepared for 100,000 visitors.

ALEXANDRA PALACE THEATRE.—Manager, Augustus Paget.—Reopens EASTER MONDAY.—Business Manager, Mr. H. de Lancey.

ALEXANDRA PALACE THEATRE.—EASTER MONDAY.—Mr. CHAS. WYNDHAM and the full company of the Criterion Theatre in THE CANDIDATE. And on Tuesday.

Easter 1885

BUSHEY
HEATH

By-Pass

ELSTREE

Corum

Watford

Brockley Hill

BROCKLEY
HILL

Barnet

Road

Barnet

Totter

**Finchley (Church End)
to Bushey Heath
Opening Winter 1940**

Way

Watfor

The

Ridge

London Rd

STANMORE

Stanmore Hill

Marsh La

Honeypot

CANONS
PARK

Whitchurch L

High St

Hale La

Watling

Av

EDGWARE

MILL HILL
(THE HALE)

MILL H.
EAST

High Rd

BURNT OAK
(WATLING)

Mollison Way

Streatfield Rd

QUEENSBURY

Watford

Welsh
Harp

COLINDALE

Colindale

Colin Av

Edgware Rd

Great Nor

Way

HEN
CENT

Rd Road

Hendon

North

BRENT

Section of a map published around 1937, showing
proposed extensions to the Underground system in
the form of a broken line, together with approximate
dates as to when they were expected to open.
Highgate (Archway) to East Finchley, opened as
planned in the Summer of 1939, but the continuation
to High Barnet was delayed until April 1940. The
former GNR Edgware branch was opened to tube
trains as far as Mill Hill East in May 1941, but the
section beyond was eventually abandoned, as was
the unfinished extension to Bushey Heath. (Author's
Collection)

Broadway

WEMBLEY PARK

Av. Ports La.

Baker Street
(Bakerloo ser

HIGH BARNET

COCKFOSTERS

ENFIELD WEST
(OAKWOOD)

Station Rd.

Cat Hill

Bramley Rd.

Enfield Rd. Slades Hill

East Finchley
to Barnet
Opening Winter 1939

TTERIDGE
HETSTONE

Lane

High Rd.

Oakleigh
North

Road

South

SOUTHGATE

Bourne Hill

Hedge

ARNOS
GROVE

VOODSIDE
PARK

High St.

Woodhouse Rd.

High Rd.

Bowes

BOUNDS GRI

WEST
NCHLEY

Nether

Ballards

Lane

High

Circular

Bounds Green Road

High

Road

FINCHLEY
(CHURCH END)

Drayton Park to
East Finchley and
Alexandra Palace
Opening Autumn
1940

ALEXANDRA
PALACE

Regent's PK

East

North

End

Road

Fortis Green

MUSWELL
HILL

Turnpike

Park Rd.

La.

EAST
FINCHLEY

CRANLEY
GARDENS

Green

GOLDERS
GREEN

Falloden Way

Finchley Rd.

Aylmer Rd.

Archway

HIGHGATE

STROUD
GREEN

Road

Highgate (Archway)
to East Finchley
Opening Summer
1939

CROUCH
END

North End Rd.

Hampstead

ey Road
anmore)

Heath

HIGHGATE
(ARCHWAY)

Junction Rd.

Holloway

Stroud

FINSBURY
PARK

Seven

94.   Here we look towards the buffer stops in the 1930s, with class N2/1 0-6-2T No.4747 about
depart for Finsbury Park. A run-round loop, sometimes used in push-pull days for temporary sto
storage can be seen to the right of the locomotive. (Lens of Sutton)

95.   Class N1 0-6-2T No. 4587 awaits departure with a train for King's Cross in the 1930s. I
the early years of the twentieth century, the original wooden platforms were in a poor conditio
so the station was rebuilt with a single island, and umbrella style awning, as shown in the
views. (H.C.Casserley)

96.   As part of the celebrations commemorating fifty years of *'The Flying Scotsman'* service between King's Cross and Edinburgh, the LNER staged an exhibition at Alexandra Palace on 14th and 15th September 1938. The locomotives on display comprised 4-6-2 No.4903 *'Peregrine'* of the 'A4' class, and restored Stirling 4-2-2 No.1 of 1870. (G.T.Stamp / G.W.Goslin Collection)

97.   Class N2/4 0-6-2T No. 2663 simmers between duties on 11th April 1945. Through services to and from Central London had ceased in September 1942, so by this time branch trains only travelled as far as Finsbury Park. (H.C.Casserley)

98.   A general view of Alexandra Palace station from the London end in 1949, shows the lineside cabling erected for the aborted Northern Line Extension to the left, and the run-round loop, sometimes used as a siding to the right. (Lens of Sutton)

99.   This is Alexandra Palace station not long before closure, with some of the platform lamps no longer in use, and the platform seat in need of repair. (Stations UK)

101.   Looking towards the buffer stops from beneath the awning, we see a crossover to the right, together with a lever frame, which was used when non-push-pull sets were in operation, and locomotives of in-coming trains need to run round their stock. (Stations UK)

1. 2. 3. 4. 5. 6. 7. 8. 9.

L. & N. E. R.

ALEXANDRA PALACE ST'N

Admit ONE to Platform 1d.

This Ticket must be given up on leaving Platform
Available for one hour. For Conditions see back

5. 6. 7. 8. 9. 10. 11. 12.

10. 11. 12.

1882

L. N. E. R.

NOT TRANSFERABLE. This ticket is issued
subject to the General Notices, Regulations
and Conditions in the Company's current Time
Tables, Book of Regulations and Bills.
Available for three days, including day of issue

ALEXANDRA PALACE ST'N to

STROUD GREEN

Fare   S   5d.
THIRD   /   11   \   CLASS
            STROUD GREEN

1418   1418

G.   N.   R.

ALEXANDRA PALACE STATION to
Alexandra Palace Stn.   Alexandra Palace Stn.

CROUCH END

CROUCH END   CROUCH END

Fare 4d Second Class Fare 4d
SEE CONDITIONS ON BACK.

4510   0154

L. N. E. R.   L. N. E. R.
For conditions   For conditions
see back   see back

Available on day of   Available on day of
issue only.   issue only.

Alexandra Palace   Alexandra Palace
ALEXANDRA PALACE ST'N to

HIGHGATE

HIGHGATE   HIGHGATE

3rd. 2½d.P   3rd. 2½d.P

2302   2302

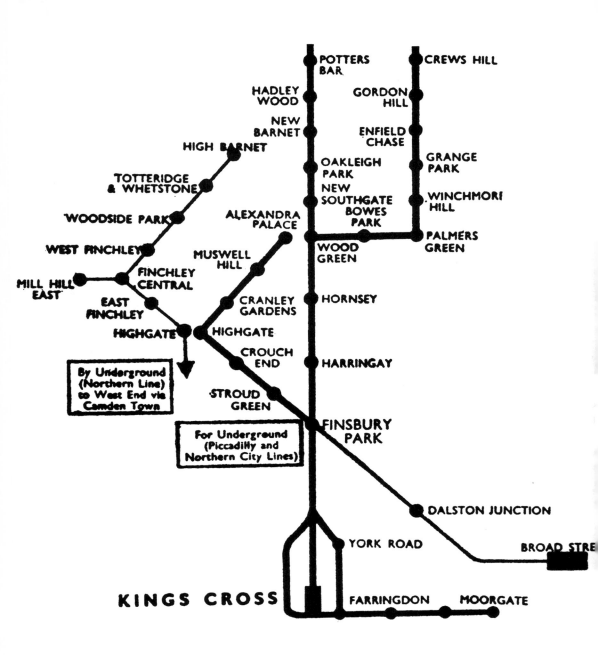

BRITISH RAILWAYS
LONDON SUBURBAN LINES
ROUTE DIAGRAM

1950

102. The two-car push-pull set for Finsbury Park departs from Alexandra Palace propelled by a class N7 0-6-2T in the early 1950s. The signal arms to the left referred to the platform roads, whilst that to the right was for the adjoining siding. (Lens of Sutton)

103. The street level building is viewed from The Avenue shortly before closure, with steps leading to the Palace terrace on the left. (Lens of Sutton)

104.   Push-pull fitted N7s, based on a Great Eastern Railway design of 1914, began to appear on branch services in later days. Here, N7/3 0-6-2T No.69699 runs into the terminus with the push-pull from Finsbury Park in the early 1950s. Push-pull workings, other than railmotors, were hardly known on Great Northern metals until their introduction onto the Alexandra Palace services in 1942. Three sets of coaches were initially employed, with vehicles coming from the Scottish area, the North East, and the former GER. According to a report in *The Railway Observer*, one of the latter, ex-Great Eastern third No.61570, was recorded as being on the line in 1953, painted in a livery of olive green. (Lens of Sutton)

North London Railway

TO

Alexandra Palace

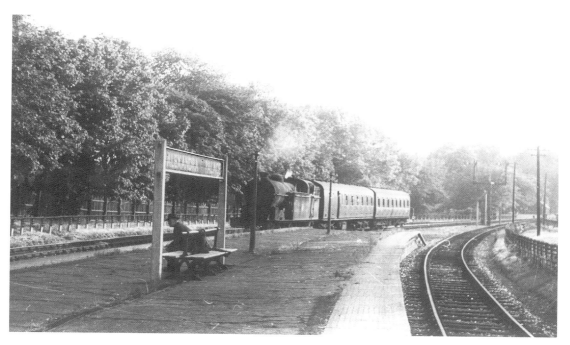

105.   A solitary passenger waits on the platform seat as non-condensing class N2/1 0-6-2T No.69519 arrives with a train from Finsbury Park on 22nd June 1954. (H.C.Casserley)

106.   No. 69519, having run round, awaits to take her two coaches back to Finsbury Park. A watchman, armed with a red flag, was on duty at the station during the final weeks, as part of a retaining wall had begun to collapse. (Connor & Butler Collection)

107. Class N2/1 0-6-2T No. 69519 sets off from the terminus shortly before closure. This locomotive
was destined to haul the last passenger train on the branch, as seen in view 112 (Author's Collection).

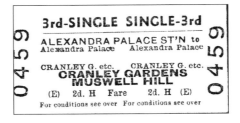

3rd-SINGLE SINGLE-3rd

ALEXANDRA PALACE ST'N to
Alexandra Palace   Alexandra Palace

CRANLEY G. etc.   CRANLEY G. etc.
CRANLEY GARDENS
MUSWELL HILL
(E)   2d. H   Fare   2d. H   (E)
For conditions see over For conditions see over

0459   0459

108.   Photographers begin to gather on the last day, as a class N2 prepares to run round its train, having just arrived from Finsbury Park. The fireman is in the process of walking forward to operate the ground frame levers seen on the left. (Alan A.Jackson)

109.   A few minutes later and the driver will stop as soon as the locomotive has cleared the crossover. He will then wait until the fireman has reset the crossover and returned to the footplate. The wooden staging to the left is possibly part of an original platform. (Alan A.Jackson)

110.   The station is seen from the terrace on the last day, with a bunker-first N2 waiting to leave with two coaches for Finsbury Park. Both crossover points were operated from the same lever frame. (Alan A. Jackson)

111.   Enthusiasts gather around class N2/4 0-6-2T No.69571 during the line's final hours as a passenger route. Inevitably someone appears to be seeking a footplate ride! (Author's Collection)

112.   The last regular passenger train for Finsbury Park blasts away from Alexandra Palace behind class N2/1 0-6-2T No.69519. Instead of the two-car formation, which normally sufficed towards the end, the train was strengthened to eight and was crowded in both directions. The locomotive carried an improvised headboard lettered *'The Alley Pally'*, and her left side tank had the BR symbol crossed out, with the legend *'Great Northern'* scribbled above in chalk. The final run was not without incident, as the train was delayed at Highgate because of a fractured drawbar beneath the leading coach. The situation was remedied by commandeering another N2 from a freight train which was following, and buffering her up to the rear. The second loco successfully propelled the crippled ensemble into the terminus, where she was taken off, and presumably sent back to her waiting wagons. Once at Alexandra Palace, 69519 ran round her stock, then coupled onto the opposite end for the return journey. This was far less eventful, and the locomotive with her eight vehicles full of enthusiasts and other interested individuals finally pulled into Finsbury Park just thirty-five minutes late. (E. Neve)

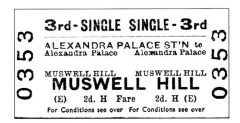

Passengers plan to run their own trains

FORMER passengers plan to reopen a shut-down railway line and run the trains themselves.

The service, known locally as the "pull and push," ran from Alexandra Palace to Finsbury Park until July last year. British Railways closed it because it did not pay.

Now the North London Passengers Protection Association plans to form a limited company to run trains over the line — with the passengers as shareholders.

Buses inadequate

Mr. Thomas Herbert, the Association's barrister secretary, said yesterday: "We are confident we can squash any objections London Transport may have. Any inquiry would show that the bus services are inadequate."

Provisional plans are for a diesel engine service from Alexandra Palace to Highgate, a four-station, five-minute journey, to link up with the Northern Line to the City and West End.

"The staff needed would be negligible," said Mr. Herbert. "We would have no ticket offices—just a conductor and driver for each train. For the shareholders there would be reduced fares.

"Any profit we make will be ploughed back to consolidate the service. Four thousand people have said they would use the line each day. British Railways said they carried only 700. I think we certainly backed a winner."

Train on H.P.

Support has been pledged from railwaymen's unions, and a diesel engine has been promised by an industrial firm. The new railway company would hire the train and eventually buy it on hire-purchase.

Mr. Herbert added: "Present rush-hour bus services force people to walk long distances and many are bringing out their cars and motor-cycles, adding to traffic congestion.

"I don't see how the Ministry of Transport can refuse to let us re-open the line—it is a national asset that is going begging."

The association is pressing for British Railways to re-open and electrify the old "pull and push." If they don't—then the Transport Minister will receive the private enterprise railway plan.

113.   A view from the platform end, looking towards Highgate on 3rd July 1954. (E. Neve)

PUSH AND PULL

OFFICIAL JOURNAL OF

NORTH LONDON PASSENGERS PROTECTION ASSOCIATION LTD.

(BY GUARANTEE)

COMMITTEE .
T. C. HURRELL, (CHAIRMAN)
G. H. PETERS, (TREASURER)
H. G. PERCY,
J. G. WILLIS,
R. B. RANKIN,
D. W. BROWN,
J. HERBERT, (MRS.)

No. 1.

Registered Office :

156, STRAND, (1st floor)
LONDON, W.C.2

October 1954.

SECRETARY :
T. A. HERBERT, LL.B.

TELEPHONE :
TEMPLE BAR
6222-8387

All communications to be addressed to the Secretary.

"Here's freedom to them that would read,
  Here's freedom to them that would write!
There's none ever feared that the truth
    should be heard
But they whom the truth would indite".
                                        (Burns).

The partially completed census of the passengers who actually used the Alexandra Palace to Finsbury Park branch railway shows the falseness of the British Transport's statements that only 700 ever used the line.

Census of 500 houses in the district so far analysed - up to the end of September 1954 - with many more to follow :-

No of adults who used train	Would use if frequent service	Those who would use late trains	Frequent visitors to houses	TOTAL
863	1,149	629	1,799	4,430

More are arriving which have not been analysed as yet! Will those who have not returned their forms please do so as soon as possible?

Have you made your protest! If not why not? There's nothing to lose but queues!

114.   After closure, the platform buildings at Alexandra Palace station lingered on for around two years before they were demolished. This view is thought to date from 1956. (Stephenson Locomotive Society)

116.   The 'Poplar & Edgware' railtour was organised by the Locomotive Club of Great Britain, and ran on 5th May 1956. It originated from Broad Street, and was hauled by North London Railway 0-6-0T No.58859 to Millwall Junction, where LMSR 'Jinty' 0-6-0T No.47484 took over. The train then travelled by way of East Ham, Forest Gate and Victoria Park to Canonbury, where the class N2 backed-on for a run through Finsbury Park to the Northern Heights. Although the route to Muswell Hill was still open to freight at the time, lifting must have been thought imminent, as an announcement in the *Railway Magazine* stated that it would travel on the branch *"if the track is still in position"*. In fact, the tour did visit the line, and proved to be its last passenger train. This view shows the approach to the terminus, with the signal post in the foreground looking very sad indeed, and No. 69506 in the process of running round. (Dr. E. Course)

Class N2/1 0-6-2T No. 69506
...ds near the branch terminus
...the 'Poplar & Edgware' Tour.
...M. Casserley)

117.   The approach to the terminus about 1956, with the derelict signal box to the left, and the Palace complete with BBC television mast on the right. (Stephenson Locomotive Society)

118.   Here we see the street level building at Alexandra Palace during the period when part of the former station site accommodated a British Rail Research Laboratory, whilst another section was used for car auctions. (J.E.Connor)

119. The overgrown platform is viewed from the terrace on 3rd July 1958, four years to the day after the departure of the last timetabled train. The track was soon to be lifted. (Alan A. Jackson)

120. Whilst the Palace was being renovated after the July 1980 fire, the opportunity was taken to restore the old station building, for use as a community centre. In this form is still survives, and provides an unassuming memorial to a branch which, had it not been for World War II, would have been part of today's Underground system. (J.E.Connor)

MP Middleton Press

Easebourne Lane, Midhurst, West Sussex. GU29 9AZ Tel: 01730 813169 Fax: 01730 812601

...WRITE OR PHONE FOR OUR LATEST LIST...

BRANCH LINES
Branch Line to Allhallows
Branch Lines to Alton
Branch Lines around Ascot
Branch Line to Ashburton
Branch Lines around Bodmin
Branch Line to Bude
Branch Lines around Canterbury
Branch Line to Cheddar
Branch Lines to East Grinstead
Branch Lines to Effingham Junction
Branch Line to Fairford
Branch Line to Hawkhurst
Branch Line to Hayling
Branch Lines to Horsham
Branch Line to Ilfracombe
Branch Lines to Longmoor
Branch Line to Lyme Regis
Branch Line to Lynton
Branch Lines around Midhurst
Branch Line to Minehead
Branch Lines to Newport (IOW)
Branch Line to Padstow
Branch Lines around Plymouth
Branch Lines around Portmadoc 1923-46
Branch Lines around Porthmadog 1954-94
Branch Lines to Seaton & Sidmouth
Branch Line to Selsey
Branch Lines around Sheerness
Branch Line to Southwold
Branch Line to Swanage
Branch Line to Tenterden
Branch Lines to Torrington
Branch Line to Upwell
Branch Lines around Wimborne
Branch Lines around Wisbech

SOUTH COAST RAILWAYS
Ashford to Dover
Brighton to Eastbourne
Chichester to Portsmouth
Dover to Ramsgate
Portsmouth to Southampton
Ryde to Ventnor
Worthing to Chichester

SOUTHERN MAIN LINES
Bromley South to Rochester
Charing Cross to Orpington
Crawley to Littlehampton
Dartford to Sittingbourne
East Croydon to Three Bridges
Epsom to Horsham
Exeter to Barnstaple
Exeter to Tavistock
Faversham to Dover
Haywards Heath to Seaford
London Bridge to East Croydon
Orpington to Tonbridge
Sittingbourne to Ramsgate
Swanley to Ashford
Tavistock to Plymouth
Victoria to Bromley South
Waterloo to Windsor

Woking to Portsmouth
Woking to Southampton
Yeovil to Exeter

COUNTRY RAILWAY ROUTES
Bath to Evercreech Junction
Bournemouth to Evercreech Jn.
Burnham to Evercreech Junction
Croydon to East Grinstead
East Kent Light Railway
Fareham to Salisbury
Frome to Bristol
Guildford to Redhill
Porthmadog to Blaenau
Reading to Basingstoke
Reading to Guildford
Redhill to Ashford
Salisbury to Westbury
Strood to Paddock Wood
Taunton to Barnstaple
Westbury to Bath
Woking to Alton
Yeovil to Dorchester

GREAT RAILWAY ERAS
Ashford from Steam to Eurostar
Festiniog in the Fifties
Festiniog in the Sixties

LONDON SUBURBAN RAILWAYS
Caterham and Tattenham Corner
Clapham Jn. to Beckenham Jn.
Crystal Palace and Catford Loop
East London Line
Finsbury Park to Alexandra Palace
Holborn Viaduct to Lewisham
Lines around Wimbledon
London Bridge to Addiscombe
Mitcham Junction Lines
North London Line
South London Line
West Croydon to Epsom
West London Line
Willesden Junction to Richmond
Wimbledon to Epsom

STEAM PHOTOGRAPHERS
O.J.Morris's Southern Railways 1919-59

STEAMING THROUGH
Steaming through Cornwall
Steaming through East Sussex
Steaming through the Isle of Wight
Steaming through Kent
Steaming through West Hants
Steaming through West Sussex

TRAMWAY CLASSICS
Aldgate & Stepney Tramways
Barnet & Finchley Tramways
Bath Tramways
Bournemouth & Poole Tramways

Brighton's Tramways
Bristol's Tramways
Camberwell & W.Norwood Tramways
Croydon's Tramways
Clapham & Streatham Tramways
Dover's Tramways
East Ham & West Ham Tramways
Eltham & Woolwich Tramways
Embankment & Waterloo Tramways
Enfield & Wood Green Tramways
Exeter & Taunton Tramways
Gosport & Horndean Tramways
Greenwich & Dartford Tramways
Hampstead & Highgate Tramways
Hastings Tramways
Holborn & Finsbury Tramways
Ilford & Barking Tramways
Kingston & Wimbledon Tramways
Lewisham & Catford Tramways
Liverpool Tramways 1. Eastern Routes
Maidstone & Chatham Tramways
North Kent Tramways
Portsmouth's Tramways
Reading Tramways
Seaton & Eastbourne Tramways
Southampton Tramways
Southend-on-sea Tramways
Southwark & Deptford Tramways
Stamford Hill Tramways
Thanet's Tramways
Victoria & Lambeth Tramways
Walthamstow & Leyton Tramways
Wandsworth & Battersea Tramways

TROLLEYBUS CLASSICS
Croydon's Trolleybuses
Hastings Trolleybuses
Maidstone Trolleybuses
Woolwich & Dartford Trolleybuses

WATERWAY ALBUMS
Hampshire Waterways
Kent and East Sussex Waterways
London's Lost Route to the Sea
London to Portsmouth Waterway
Surrey Waterways

MILITARY BOOKS
Battle over Portsmouth
Battle over Sussex 1940
Blitz over Sussex 1941-42
Bombers over Sussex 1943-45
Bognor at War
Military Defence of West Sussex
Secret Sussex Resistance

OTHER BOOKS
Brickmaking in Sussex
Garraway Father & Son
Index to all Stations
Industrial Railways of the South East
London Chatham & Dover Railway

SOUTHERN RAILWAY VIDEO
War on the Line